AF208030

MAKE SOMEONE HAPPY

Bob Wendorf, Psy.D.

Psych Savvy Books
Birmingham, Alabama

Published by: Psych Savvy Books
Birmingham, Alabama

ISBN 0-9677943-0-7

Copyright © 2000 Bob Wendorf, Psy. D.
All rights reserved

To obtain copies of this book, please E-mail
Bob Wendorf, Psy. D. at Psychsavvy@ aol.com

This book is dedicated to my wife Margaret –
who makes me happy.

MAKE SOMEONE HAPPY

Contents

Part I. MAKE SOMEONE HAPPY

MAKE SOMEONE HAPPY

Bob Wendorf

A psychologist is, as much as anything, a teacher. I try to teach my patients how to clean up the messes in their lives, relate more effectively to others and to be happy. Over the years I've collected or assembled a set of mini-lectures I deliver to my patients. I've tried to gather most of them together in one place, which is this book. As a therapist I use whatever works, from whatever source, so these little talks come from a wide variety of people, places, books, and clinical experiences. I've tried to credit the sources when I knew them, but over the years one forgets what is borrowed and what is one's own. Thus, I apologize if I've inadvertently taken credit for somebody else's thoughts.

There are a number of stories in the book that come from my clinical practice. The patients I've discussed are real people with the real problems I've described. However, I've changed names and some details, even swapped particulars around a bit, to protect their privacy.

I might even have embellished a tale some, after years of retelling, forgetting or "enhancing" a story. But they're basically true. Some are sad, some comical, but I hope all are presented with a basic respect for people doing the best they can in some bad situations.

I am grateful to my wife Margaret for helping

me assemble the book and get it published. I am grateful to my patients, who taught me what clinical psychology is really about. And I am deeply indebted to my parents for giving me love and discipline and support. What I know about being happy comes mostly from them.

Part I MAKE SOMEONE HAPPY
Chapter One. Making Yourself Happy:

Everybody wants to be happy. Some people try to earn happiness, others to steal it. Some folks are only happy if they're miserable. Some have given up on ever being happy, but they still desire it. Everybody wants to gain happiness, but unfortunately, a lot of people aren't very good at it. The Declaration of Independence guarantees your right to pursue it, but not necessarily to catch it. And, of course, no one is happy all the time. Life just isn't set up that way.

Why isn't it? Why can't we just naturally be happy, without any particular effort on our own parts? Actually, it does seem to work nearly that way for some people, who seem to glide effortlessly through life, eternally optimistic and always happy. I suspect that often we just don't see what happens in privacy or behind the scenes for these folks, but I'll admit that happiness comes a lot easier for some than others. Still, I think the need to pursue happiness in life is built-in to the nature of reality. Succeeding at something feels really good only if the task was arduous enough to count for something. Conflict and strife are built-in to relationships, and mitigate against the happiness we derive from them. You can't enjoy the happiness of being a hero without slaying some sort of a dragon. There's no winner without a loser, no champion without an also-ran, no success without failure. Happiness exists in contrast to unhappiness. In a world without evil there's also no good.

That's part of what the Book of Genesis is about. When the human species evolved to the level of self-awareness, it was forever doomed to work at being happy. Eating from the Tree of the Knowledge of Good and Evil made us aware of our unhappiness as well as our happiness. A tiger in the jungle is incapable of either good or evil because he is not aware of himself as an actor on life's stage. If a tiger eats you, that's not an evil deed; he's just doing what comes naturally. If he doesn't eat you it isn't an act of charity; he just ain't hungry. A tiger is programmed by instinct, not directed by his own choices. Thus, he feels pleasure, but not happiness, pain, but not the "agony of defeat." Human beings, being self-aware, are also responsible for their actions, as well as their feelings. Thus, we're responsible for making ourselves happy.

It would be foolhardy to present a specific recipe for happiness. Everyone's formula is bound to be a little different from others, and what works for one person won't help another one bit. But it is possible to outline some broad strategies for being happy and at least to rule out some approaches that definitely won't work. That's what this book is about.

There's an ironic little truism that I rather like: "Happiness," it is said, "is self-induced." That's right. In the first place, happiness is an emotion, a feeling, inside of you. Thus, like all feelings, it is produced by your nervous system, by your brain in conjunction with your hormones. No one else can reach into your body and adjust your emotional generator to the "happy" setting. More importantly, happiness is the byproduct of your actions and thoughts. It's not automatic and it doesn't just happen. You must *do* something, even if only to think the right thoughts, to make yourself happy. Someone else can say or do something in hopes of pleasing you or bringing you happiness, but you still have to make yourself happy with what the other person's done. Who has never had the experience of giving someone a gift only to find he/she isn't happy with it? Who hasn't had to work at being happy with what he's gotten instead of feeling disappointed when he didn't get what he wanted for Christmas?

Looked at in this way, it seems a simplistic, even trivial point: **you make your own happiness**. Yet many people believe quite differently about happiness and often end up quite unhappy as a result. For example, many people believe it is the job of some other person to make them happy. It may be a spouse, a boss, a parent, but it is *their* responsibility. People who believe this typically end up feeling angry and disappointed instead, as the other often refuses to cooperate or fails to produce.

This is what "mid-life crises" are about. You turn forty only to realize that you aren't happy. Since you married your wife so she'd make you happy, you assume that she is to blame when you're not. Obviously, she isn't doing her job as she's supposed to. So you get a divorce and find another, younger, woman to make you happy. Some men run through several of these before they realize it is themselves they are truly unhappy with. They've turned an identity crisis into a marital crisis, and failed to resolve either of them.

It is widely believed that happiness is the result of what happens to you and is therefore in the hands of fate or luck. But we often have little or no control over events, over what happens to us. If it were true that what happens to us determines our happiness, we wouldn't be responsible for our happiness, but we also wouldn't be able to do much about it. Yet it is evident that some people aren't at all happy, despite a life full of apparently happy-type events. In my practice I see a lot of rich, successful and healthy people who are thoroughly depressed, anxious, or angry. On the other hand, some people manage to be quite happy in circumstances others would find utterly intolerable. How can this be? How, for example, could the famous "Bird Man of Alcatraz" fashion a happy life while incarcerated, with no hope of parole, in a notoriously unpleasant prison? Why do movie and rock music stars kill themselves?

Happiness and Rational Thinking:

The answer lies partly in the nature of emotions. Psychologists (notably Albert Ellis, David Burns, and Aaron Beck) tell us that if isn't what happens to us that causes us to feel one way or another, it's what we *think* about what happens that determines our emotions. As Shakespeare put it, "Nothing's either good or bad, but thinking makes it so." The emotion isn't directly caused by the event, but rather by one's interpretation of the event. ("Thinking" is defined a bit broadly here, to include ideas but also visual images, memories, and imaginings.)

According to this theory, it is these "cognitive mediators," these thoughts in between the event and the feeling, that really cause our emotional responses. Perhaps getting slapped in the face is an exception to the rule. It doesn't take a lot of thinking to conclude that it hurts, and most people will react with instantaneous angry feelings. But even here there's room for interpretation of the event and its meaning, and the resulting emotion will vary accordingly. If the slapper is a lot bigger than the slappee, the latter might feel not so much angry as fearful. Or if the victim is a man who's just made a lewd comment to the woman who slapped him, he might be feeling more shame or humiliation than anger. And certainly, if you're still angry two weeks later, it would be illogical to attribute this anger to the slapping event per se. Clearly, you're angry now because you're *thinking* about the slap, not because of the slap itself. If your interpretation or thought about an event changes, so does your emotional response. You're walking through the mall and feel a hard slap on the back, as you hear someone calling you an "old son of a bitch." You wheel around in anger, ready to strike back, only to find it's an old buddy greeting you. "S.O.B." turns out to be a term of endearment, not an insult, in the peculiar way some men show each other affection. You now grin happily and punch him back with an equally vulgar pet name, but without rancor. The event has changed in your mind, and so has the feeling associated with it.

Further, as Dr. Ellis stresses, if you're experiencing sustained, continuing negative emotions, there must be something wrong with your thinking. Ellis says in this case your thought is invariably irrational or illogical as well as, obviously, dysfunctional. You may be catastrophizing, for example, telling yourself something is "awful" when more realistically it's merely "unpleasant" or "unfortunate." Or you may be overgeneralizing, telling yourself that no one loves you simply because you got turned down for one date. I've seen dozens of attempted suicides following the break up of a love affair. These people are telling themselves they no longer have a reason to live and that no one will ever love them, both irrational ideas, but both powerful emotional stimulants.

Contrariwise, I've heard sales people advised to be happy when a potential customer says, "no."

Since it takes one hundred rejections to make one sale, each turn-down is a step towards an eventual success and therefore cause for celebration! This may be a bit Pollyanna-ish but, it's probably an essential way of thinking for a happy salesperson.

So, one way in which you make yourself happy is to think thoughts which produce happy feelings (and, of course eliminate or change thoughts which cause unhappy emotions.)

Cognitive therapists like Ellis and Beck provide a catalogue of some of the most common irrational, dysfunctional ideas, which lead to emotional distress. One is the idea, noted above, that it is awful and catastrophic when things don't go our way. Actually, it is rarely disastrous and sometimes downright beneficial not to get what you want or to have things go a bit awry. Let's say you're running to catch a bus but arrive too late, just as the bus is pulling away. This is frustrating, annoying, unpleasant and inconvenient. You'll have to wait for the next bus (which may be twenty minutes), take a cab (expensive and hard to find) or maybe walk (tiring but good exercise). Maybe you'll be late or miss your event altogether. But unless you're headed for emergency surgery, in which case you should be in an ambulance, you won't die from missing the bus. It's unpleasant, but not awful. If, on the other hand, you're running to catch the bus, miss it, and arrive just in time to get run over - that's awful. This is the standard I suggest for comparing life events to, in order to determine if they are awful or merely unpleasant: If you miss the bus, that's unpleasant; if the bus doesn't miss you, that's awful. And if it's truly awful you're entitled to a major tantrum or fit. If it's merely unpleasant, then get annoyed or chagrined, but leave rage and despair for the truly catastrophic. What will determine your emotions is what you tell yourself about the event. If you think it's awful, that's how it'll feel.

Actually, it can even be beneficial to have events go wrong. In the bus example you may end up getting health-enhancing exercise, as well as a colorful and instructive tour of the city. If nothing else, being frustrated in your desires builds character and develops coping skills you'll need when something really bad does happen. People who always get what they want end up being spoiled, miserable people who are universally disliked.

Another irrational idea is that it is essential to be liked by virtually everyone you meet. This idea is dysfunctional because it will cause you great distress whenever someone doesn't like you, will lead to great and undue anxiety in relationships and may lead you into self-defeating ways of gaining love and approval (see below). It is essential to be liked by somebody at some time in your life in order to develop social skills and to believe in your own like-ability. We are social animals and "everybody needs somebody sometimes." But there is truly no need to be liked by *everyone*. Furthermore, this idea is irrational because it demands the impossible. It is inevitable that you will eventually be disliked by someone, even if you're a sweetheart and a saint. There are some people who won't like you simply because you have blond hair. If you dye it black, then some other person won't like you. Some people out there don't like anybody, and they won't like you either! You may even be disliked by someone because you resemble his Aunt Maudie, who beat him when he was little, a transference of feelings he may be completely unaware of. Even if you pretended to be someone you're not, the best you could hope for would be to have that false self or role loved. But that's not you. You can't make people like you; that's at their discretion, not yours. A more rational idea would be that everybody needs to be loved, but not to be loved by everybody. If someone doesn't like you, it is unfortunate, but not awful. It doesn't mean that you're not lovable or will never be loved, just that this person at this moment doesn't like you. That's a shame, but it's not a tragedy.

Similarly, there are people who believe it's necessary to be "the best" in everything they do. Otherwise, they cannot feel good about themselves. These individuals fail to distinguish between second place and last. If you're not the very best, you're a complete loser. This is irrational on the face of it, but also quite dysfunctional. Again you ask the impossible of yourself, if you believe this idea. There's only one "best" in anything and chances are it's not you. If you're the best now, how will you feel when another takes your place, as will inevitably happen? If you're the best high school basketballer in your state, will you still be the best on a college team? In the NBA? This idea dooms you to feel like a failure, even if you're one of the brightest, most talented people in the world. I had a friend in graduate school who confessed to me that he was miserable and hated himself. He was one of the best students in one of the best graduate programs in the country, as well as one of the most popular. On a campus obsessed with racquetball he was ranked in the top twenty. His loving wife had been Miss Whatever State. But he wasn't *the best* student, *the best liked,* the *top* racquetballer, or married to Miss America. So in his own eyes, he was a loser. He told me he was beginning to recognize how crazy his thinking was, a notion I was happy to confirm. When he truly learned to quit thinking this way, he became a lot happier.

Perfectionism:

In the same vein, **perfectionists** believe that in order to value and respect themselves they must perform perfectly in some or all areas of their lives. They may hold others to this standard as well. These poor folks are just as doomed as the ones described above because the achievement of perfection is logically impossible to living beings. The very hallmark of life is change; it is in constant motion. Change must either be an improvement (in which case you weren't perfect) or a regression (in which case you aren't perfect now). Either way perfection is impossible. Perfection is a steady state, possible (if at all) only in death. This is part of what Browning meant in saying "A man's reach should exceed his grasp, or what's a heaven for?" The perfectionist has set herself up to fail. And failure can lead to unhappiness.

Beyond this, perfection as a goal seems to me undesirable for other reasons. To me, much of the fun in life is in learning new things, in growing and developing as a person. If you could actually achieve perfection your growth would instantly cease and you'd learn nothing new (because growth would be an improvement, and you can't improve on perfection). We learn more from our mistakes than from our triumphs. Do something perfectly a thousand times over and you learn only about boredom. Screw it up and you learn something new, painfully perhaps, but still new growth.

Besides this, perfectionism soon becomes negativism. If something is 98% good, the perfectionist focuses only on the other 2%. This is the area that needs improving because it is "bad" in some way. Perfectionists see themselves as nobly pursuing a glorious goal, but in practice they are always looking at what is wrong, bad, ugly, or otherwise short of perfection. This is negativism, and leads to low self-esteem and a tendency to criticize others. Woe to the child of a perfectionist who'll never do anything well enough to please his parent. It's OK to strive for perfection, but you should value and enjoy the effort without expecting and demanding success.

These are only a few of the countless ways people make themselves unhappy by thinking irrationally. Some of us think it is necessary to dwell on possible unpleasant events and worry about them occurring. Some become preoccupied with thoughts of revenge for past injuries (which only keeps you up at night and doesn't hurt the other person at all). Some people simply depress themselves by selectively looking only at the down sides of life, looking at what they haven't got instead of counting their blessings. It is probably universal to have some thought process which causes chronic unhappiness, anxiety or resentment. But a major key to living a happy life is to uncover these ideas and learn to rethink them. This is the "power of positive thinking."

Worrying:
Worrying is another dysfunctional thought pattern I frequently encounter in my work as a therapist. Worrying is distressing; it feels bad. It also accomplishes nothing, because it doesn't change reality or even lead to a process of change. Worrying means stewing and fretting over events which haven't even happened yet or which are in the past and therefore unchangeable. Worrying means living an unpleasant event in your imagination and that means experiencing the painful

emotions associated with that event. Often people are worrying about things they have no control over: whether somebody likes them, whether war will break out in the Middle East, whether the Braves will win the Pennant. Many people worry so much and so emotionally that the event or circumstance they're worrying about pales by comparison . . . if it even occurs at all. I've seen people worry themselves into a true panic attack over such trivialities as making a blunder in a speech. I personally have blundered in many speeches and find it can indeed be a bit embarrassing, especially if you take yourself too seriously. But that's all. Despite popular thinking, nobody actually dies of embarrassment. Panic attacks, in contrast, can be completely incapacitating. There's no comparison. What a shame to waste mental energy and experience emotional distress over something that may not happen at all and at worst isn't as bad as the worrying itself. Further, worrying causes anxiety, and anxiety produces autonomic arousal which can become harmful to your health. Worrying can raise blood pressure, cause headaches, even contribute to the development of ulcers.

It is important to distinguish here between worrying and problem-solving. The former is dysfunctional and distressing; the latter is a very useful and productive form of thought. Worrying goes nowhere, but problem-solving can lead to effective solutions and therefore increased happiness. How do you tell the difference? Worrying focuses on the problem: "What if so and so happens? Oh, I hope she isn't angry. What'll I do if I get sick? Wouldn't it be awful if ...?" Problem-solving focuses instead on solutions: "How can I protect myself in this situation? How can I earn the money I need? What's the best way to solve this problem?"

If you find yourself circling around and around a problem . . . i. e. worrying . . . switch your thinking to problem-solving instead. It'll feel a lot better and be a lot more constructive. Sometimes you won't be able to think of a solution that seems workable or doesn't have undesirable side-effects. In that case, a partial solution is to resolve to research the problem or consult with a professional who can help you develop a more useful plan of action. This is often enough to give a sense of relief and get the problem off your mind. At times you may come across a problem that simply has no solution. In this case, stop thinking about the problem. You'll accomplish nothing except to make yourself miserable. Switch your thoughts to something else. Some people seem to feel morally obligated to worry about certain things. For example, it is unfortunately all too common in some third world countries to experience civil wars in which thousands of people die of starvation. That's a pretty awful thought, and it makes you feel bad to think of it. But I haven't got the money to feed these people, and if I could send a plane load of food over, the rebel army would shoot it down. I can give to relief efforts and hope for the best, but this is a problem I simply can't solve. So, cold as it may sound, it does nobody any good for me to continue to worry about it. Better to expend my efforts in a more workable direction.

Once again, right thinking comes to the rescue and leads to increased happiness. Problem-solving is productive, rational thinking while worrying makes you unhappy. It is often useful to ask yourself some critical questions about your worries or fears. Questions like, "So what?" or "What's the worst thing that could happen?" When you think it through, the worst-case scenario often turns out to be relatively manageable and only mildly unpleasant. Imagined dire consequences are often so unlikely or so exaggerated as to be unworthy of your attention. I worried terribly about getting a "C" in college and finally got one, in French. I was devastated. Yet, thirty years later I'm at a loss to see any adverse effect that grade had on my life. I worried for nothing. Similarly, I used to become quite anxious about calling a girl for a date. What if she said, "No?" Then I realized that the worst thing that could happen was that I'd end up without a date, and I *already* didn't have a date. I couldn't end up worse off and I'd be anxious until I called, so I'd go ahead and call. Of course, if being turned down meant all women found me loathsome and I'd never get a date and no one would ever love me, that would be bad. But it didn't. Getting turned down simply meant that one girl didn't want to go out with me on one night. No big deal, once you think it through logically, but it took me a fair amount of agony to figure that out.

Obsessive-Compulsive Disorder:
   Perhaps the most serious form of worrying occurs with obsessive-compulsives. These are people who become obsessively pre-occupied with certain thoughts or ideas that make them anxious. That's the obsession. In order to reduce their anxiety, they then feel compelled to act out some sort of ritual behavior which they feel protects them or makes things OK. That's the compulsion. For example, I had a patient who obsessed over the danger of giving her family food poisoning. She couldn't stop worrying about salmonella and botulism and couldn't shake the thought that her cooking would kill them all. If she so much as touched the "wrong" objects in the kitchen or dropped a crumb on the counter she would be compelled to scrub and sterilize the entire kitchen and its contents, a process that could take hours. This poor woman's entire life was dominated by these thoughts and rituals. Meanwhile, her house was a mess and her family was starving, a far greater threat than food poisoning. Other obsessive-compulsives have counting or checking rituals such as checking all the doors and window locks seven times before going to bed. Others must touch things in certain ways, arrange things in a certain order, or

30085

recite ritualized speeches to themselves. If they don't they are overwhelmed with anxiety. If they do carry out the compulsion, their anxiety is reduced for a while. Since the reduction of anxiety is rewarding, they are more motivated to repeat the behavior. Thus, there's a self-perpetuating quality to obsessive-compulsiveness.

Obsessive-compulsiveness can vary considerably, from downright useful to mildly eccentric to utterly incapacitating. It's pretty helpful for an accountant, for example, to be a bit on the compulsive side. At the other extreme, people with Obsessive-Compulsive Disorder (OCD) suffer from a true psychiatric illness and can have a horrible existence. In its most extreme forms, OCD very probably has a physiological basis, perhaps one inherited genetically. At the same time, obsessive-compulsives are also clearly victims of irrational thinking. They are looking for absolute certainty in a probabilistic universe. Perception and memory are too imprecise for anyone to be absolutely sure he unplugged the iron before leaving home. Even if you think you have a memory of pulling the plug, can you be *sure* your memory is from today and not yesterday? Checking and counting and touching rituals, not to mention incantations, are irrational attempts to gain security by magical operations. And it's irrational to spend one's time and energy obsessing about extremely unlikely events in any case.

Fortunately, obsessive-compulsive disorder is

often quite treatable, using behavioral, cognitive and medical therapies. OCD patients can learn to rethink their views and deal with life more rationally. They can learn to tolerate and cope with anxiety without using ritual behaviors. And many OCD patients derive significant relief from medications, especially the tricyclic antidepressants and serotonin re-uptake blockers such as Prozac.

Learning to think more rationally and eliminate illogical, dysfunctional thinking is essential to living a happy life. However, for most people this isn't quite enough. If you're going to be happy, it helps to have things to be happy about. Bad things happen to you quite spontaneously, through no effort or action on your part. **Good things happen mostly because you make them happen**. So it helps to do things which are likely to make you happy. Most people develop a more-or-less conscious plan for their lives, a plan which will carry out some strategy for gaining happiness. Some strategies work better than others, of course, and some don't work at all, at least in the long run. But everybody's got a plan and is trying out one or several of these strategies. Let's examine some of them more closely, with an eye to what does or doesn't work. Before we do that, however, it is necessary to take a quick look at the flip side and deal with the issues of unhappiness, sadness, and depression.

Unhappiness and Depression:

As we've already noted, it is not possible to be happy all the time. If nothing else, you have to experience some unhappiness so you'll have something to contrast happiness with. Otherwise, you might not recognize it. Besides, every human alive is going to go through some tough times sooner or later. Somebody is going to reject you, you're going to fail a test, you'll lose someone close to you, you'll fall down and hurt yourself. Pain, sadness, and grief are universal experiences, part of what makes us human and builds our character. Unhappiness and even depression are normal and healthy, if not especially desirable emotions. While it is entirely reasonable to seek to avoid as much unhappiness as possible, it is irrational to expect to avoid it all. Maximize the good times and minimize the bad. What is decidedly *not* normal is true clinical depression, although statistics indicate about one fourth of us will experience one at some time in our lives. Clinical depression is no fun and does not usually have to be tolerated forever. It is a true illness and can usually be treated.

Everybody gets down now and again, but if you hit the bottom and stay there for weeks at a time, you are clinically depressed. Depression is characterized by overwhelming feelings of sadness and unhappiness– or "anhedonia"-- lasting for long periods of time. It includes also feelings of helplessness and of worthlessness. Depressed people despair of things ever getting better. Their

life seems meaningless and worthless. They may
even have thoughts of dying or become obsessed
with suicide. Depressed people have no energy
("lethargy") and tend to lose interest in things they
normally find enjoyable. Often, they lose their
appetite as well. They even tend to lose interest in
sex ("decreased libido"). And, surprisingly,
depressed people don't sleep properly, either
sleeping excessively, or, more commonly, waking
early and finding it impossible to return to sleep. In
fact, this is the most common symptom of
depression, second only to the feeling of sadness per
se.

All this sets up a most unfortunate pattern which
tends to perpetuate the depression. Exercise is a
great anti-depressant, producing a flow of
endorphins, which is nature's own joy juice.
Endorphins are naturally occurring brain chemicals
which mimic the action of morphine, reducing pain
and enhancing feelings of pleasure. But exercise
takes energy, and depressed people have no energy.
Some of them literally can't get out of bed; they're
not going to go to the track. Likewise, eating a
good meal or having sexual relations makes you feel
better, physically as well as emotionally. But
depressed patients lose their appetite and their
libido. And they aren't interested in their friends,
hobbies or jobs, all of which might make them feel
better. Depressed people can't bring themselves to
do the very things they need to do to fight
depression. In really severe depression, even one's

thinking becomes distorted, again tending to perpetuate the depression.

Depression occurs in many degrees of severity and comes in several varieties. There are depressions which are nearly pure psychological reactions to a distressing event. Your dog dies and you feel depressed. There are other depressions that are probably purely chemical events. You experience enough sustained stress, especially emotional stress, and many people will react with a biological depression. This kind of depression seems to have a strong genetic component, running in families. So does manic-depressive illness, now renamed "bipolar disorder." Most depressions are somewhere in the middle, with both psychological and biochemical components. If they last long enough, all depressions tend to become biological. Thus, I can't over stress the idea that depression is a disease, a problem in biochemistry. It is not a moral failure or sign of weakness, but a treatable illness.

To illustrate this point, let me describe a middle-aged man I saw several years ago. When I asked about his life, he could identify nothing wrong with it. He was President of a large and prosperous business, and his wife, an artist, had just held a successful exhibition. One son was on scholarship at an Ivy League school and the other playing ball for Alabama (or was it Auburn?) His health was great, his marriage in good shape, his house paid off. Yet he sat with tears rolling down his face and described himself at the bottom of a dark pit with no visible means of escape. His was a classic biological depression. Three weeks on Prozac and he was fine. No psychotherapy, just medication.

More typically, depression includes both psychological and physiological components. Thus, both psychotherapy and medication are required for its treatment. With fairly mild depressions, psychotherapy alone may be sufficient, especially if it includes both training in rational thinking and behavioral instructions to do the things described above to fight depression. There is another kind of depression that often responds well to therapy, or perhaps therapy and a low dose of medication. This is "dysthymia" or "dysthymic disorder," the name for a chronic, low-grade depression, which can actually last a lifetime without being diagnosed. People with this disorder may be thought of as simply not knowing how to be happy. Parents teach their kids everything from tying shoes to preparing income taxes, but some of them, surprisingly, tell their offspring essentially nothing about how to be happy. Some of them probably don't know how themselves. Many dysthymics I've worked with didn't even recognize that they felt depressed. They just knew something wasn't right. These patients often do quite well with fairly straight-forward instructions and feedback. They can probably even cut their therapy time shorter by reading the rest of this book, which they are cordially invited to do.

Chapter Two. Self-Focused Strategies for Happiness
The Way of Pleasure:

There are many things in life capable of stimulating our central nervous systems in ways that feel good. Many of these things are readily available, relatively inexpensive and more or less socially acceptable. And they tend to work very quickly and reliably, providing almost immediate physical gratification. Thus, it is easy to confuse these physical pleasures with true happiness. Food, with some notable exceptions, makes your taste buds feel good. Sex makes your genitals feel good and, like food, causes a release of brain chemicals called "endorphins" which give you a warm, rosy glow all over. If you're cheating on your husband, the illicit, secret, conspiratorial and generally naughty nature of the sex adds to the emotion of excitement, which makes it even more pleasurable. Runners get their endorphin buzz in a relatively healthy way, gamblers in a potentially dangerous way. Other naturally occurring brain chemicals also provide physically pleasurable sensations: race car drivers and ER docs may be "tripping" on their own natural adrenaline.

Where naturally occurring brain chemicals are insufficient or inconvenient to the provision of pleasure, it is easy enough to supplement them artificially. Alcohol, heroin, magic mushrooms, and morning glory seeds all cause physiological changes in our brains, which are associated with highly pleasurable sensations. So compelling is the pleasure these drugs provide that for some people they become their major, indeed their only way of seeking happiness. A recovering heroin addict told me that heroin made him feel so good he simply dropped all other activities or interests. He realized eventually he had to choose between heroin and a life. He said it was a very close call. He could understand why others chose the gratification of getting high to the exclusion of all other pursuits. Even sex. A cocaine addict was confused when I asked what he did when he was "high." "You don't *do anything*," he finally said. "You just do coke."

There are other pleasures as well, probably an infinite variety of them. There's the aesthetic pleasure of a sunset or a Van Gogh, the pleasure of listening to a good jazz combo, and the pleasure of smelling a rose. All these and more can bring us a measure of happiness, and we probably all need to fill our pleasure quotas fairly regularly. Dr. Hook and the Medicine Show sang, " Some men need some killer weed, some men need cocaine. Some men need some cactus juice to purify their brain. Some men need two women, some need alcohol. Everybody needs a little something, But Lord, I need it _all_!" (Which points out the additional benefits of mixing your pleasures together.)

So "what's so bad about feeling good?" Nothing, really. It's just that pleasure-seeking is not happiness, and is often dangerous besides. The way of pleasure is always potentially addictive. The something that makes you feel orgasmically good in the short run also makes you feel suicidally bad in the long run. A crack addict is always chasing his first "high" because each succeeding one is just a little bit less intense. Each succeeding "crash" carries him a little farther down. Eventually he's at rock bottom (pun intended) hoping only to rid himself of horrible withdrawal symptoms and pull himself up to a nearly normal level of comfort. I saw a couple once who ran "crystal meth" (speed) for five days, then ran out. They felt so nervous, so edgy, so depressed, and so hostile that they trashed their apartment and threw the TV through the window. When there was nothing left to smash they beat each other up. Alcoholics kill people for the pleasure of driving crookedly and gamblers mortgage the house to make the big killing which will make them rich and happy (and get their creditors off their backs). They always lose eventually.

Pleasure isn't happiness and its compulsive pursuit tends to become self-defeating and self-destructive. Most philanderers, people who have one affair after another, eventually realize they are bored of sex, don't like persons of the opposite sex, and find their lives tawdry, empty, and meaningless. Yet they are driven compulsively to each new encounter. Pornography addicts become increasingly jaded and must find increasingly grotesque and disgusting material to excite them. Even winning at games can become tedious or perhaps not worth the price of fractured bones and broken egos. Remember the Twilight Zone episode in which a mobster is killed and wakes up in the presence of an apparent angel who gives him everything he wants, instantly on command? He draws two cards to an inside straight, breaks up a rack of pool balls, pocketing all of them and, orders up a steak and a gorgeous blonde to fall in love with him. He quickly becomes bored in this heavenly existence, complains to the "angel" and declares he really should have ended up in "the other place" instead of this apparent paradise. "I thought you knew, sir," says the angel. "This *is* the other place."

Many other pleasures are much less damaging and not so limited in their efficiency. A Renoir keeps leaping off the canvas at you and The Ninth Symphony keeps sounding better and better as I learn to listen better. Yet, I don't want to hear Beethoven every day. I'll never tire of the chicken curry "P.K." taught me to cook in 1969, though I'm not sure of its effect on my cholesterol count. These and a multitude of other pleasures enhance our lives, and, in moderation, are a legitimate source of happiness and joy. But they aren't in themselves enough to make a happy life. **Indeed, I would argue that the pursuit of and the sharing of pleasure may bring more happiness than the pleasure itself**. Pure, un-enlightened hedonism is ultimately empty, if not tiresome and down right destructive. Ask the ancient Romans. The pleasures that are more satisfying and do lead to happiness are those one must earn and often, those one must learn to appreciate. The joys of giving or of sharing a sunset with a loved one come to mind. Or, the thrill of discovering a new animal species - a thrill earned by years of hard work. In my practice, **I see many people who simply don't know how to be happy and try to fill up their emptiness with pleasure-seeking**. They are sad people indeed. Much of the pleasure-seeking I see in my clinical practice occurs on an impulsive spur- of-the-moment basis. In fact, this is probably the number one problem I deal with, and the major cause of my patients' unhappiness. All behavior has consequences. Some happen immediately, others much later; some are big, some small; some are positive and others negative. Whenever you push on the universe, the universe pushes back. The trick, then, is to act so as to maximize the positive and minimize the negative consequences. The problem is that short and long-term consequences are typically reversed. If you do something that pays off right away, chances are it will cost you later. Behavior that is highly rewarding in the long run typically has no immediate pay-off and usually it actually costs you for a while. Impulsive people can't resist the urge to get their goodies *now ,* so in the long run they end up unhappy.

To illustrate this problem, let's examine the consequences of a situation I use to teach decision-making to my impulsive patients. We start with a problem situation, in this case that you have no car.

We then "brain storm" all the possible options for solving this problem, i. e. ways of getting a car. We list the consequences for each proposed solution, scoring them + for rewarding ones and - for punishing or unpleasant ones. Finally, we add the pluses and minuses to determine which course of action produces the highest gain at the lowest cost.

For the car situation, options include buying a car, stealing a car, getting someone to give you a car, or making one. Unless you're a Henry Ford the last option is probably not a viable one, so we eliminate it from the analysis. Getting a car as a gift would be great, as there's no cost to you. Unfortunately, since this depends on somebody else's action, you can't make it happen. So this isn't really a choice either. (Borrowing, by the way, is a temporary gift, just as renting is buying by the day or month. They're covered by these other analyses). We're left with buying or stealing a car.

To buy a car you need money and that means going to work. Work isn't fun, which is why they have to pay people to do it, so we'll give it a minus score. Since it'll take a while to earn enough even for a down payment, you'll have to wait on the car. Nobody likes waiting, so that scores another minus. Then you actually have to give your hard-earned money away, to somebody at the car store. Another minus. At this point, things begin to improve: you get the car, with no hassles; it's legally yours and can't be taken from you; you're proud of your purchase and you have the respect of others for earning the car yourself. You probably will buy it on time and thereby help establish a good credit rating. All these are positives. Final score: three minuses, and six pluses.

Stealing a car comes out pretty much opposite to buying. There are three quick pluses as you get the car now, with no waiting, no working, and no money spent. Then the minuses begin to roll in. First, you're nervous, driving a "hot" vehicle. Then, since cars are hard to hide, you're busted. They take the car away and they take you to jail. There you work, you wait, you spend money on a lawyer and you try to persuade your roommate to find someone besides you for his new girlfriend. You lose your civil rights; you have a criminal record; you're rejected by society; and you feel ashamed of yourself (one hopes). The bottom line tallies to three quick pluses and at least a dozen minuses, mostly big ones. Comparing the two, buying is clearly the better option, with fewer drawbacks and more rewards. So why does anybody resort to stealing? The answer becomes clear when you look at the timing of the consequences. When you decide to buy a car, the first or short-term consequences are all bad. It only pays in the long-term. Stealing is just the reverse, a quick pay-off followed by long-term costs and punishment. Here's how the analysis looks on paper:

Problem: No Car

Options:

	1. Buy a car	2. Steal a car	3. Get a gift	4. Make a car
Consequences:	Work -	No work +	(Can't do it)	(Can't do it)
(Short-term)	Wait -	No waiting +		
	Give away money -	No money +		
---	---	---	---	---
(Long-term)	Get the car +	Scared -		
	No legal hassles +	Busted -		
	Establish credit +	Take car away -		
	Can't be taken +	Go to jail -		
	You're proud +	Work in jail -		
	Respect of others +	Wait in jail -		
		Money for lawyer -		
		Criminal Record -		
		No civil rights -		
		Bad reputation -		
		No self-respect -		
		Cell mate problems -		
Totals: 3 minuses 6 pluses		**12 minuses 3 pluses**		

Notice that in both cases the greater consequences, good or bad, happen over the long term. Either way you have to pay for what you get, but you pay less if you pay up-front. Get the goodies now and pay later, it'll cost you. It's even true in how you buy the car. A cash deal will likely include a discount, while buying it over time involves significant interest payments. That's how life works.

The impulsive person, however, acts so as to maximize his immediate pleasure. He's not concerned about the long run, just the present temptation. So in the long run, the impulsive pleasure-seeker ends up with more negatives than positives in his life, a sure recipe for unhappiness. I frequently encounter these folks in my practice. They're depressed because "later" has come and they're experiencing the negative consequences of their earlier impatient misconduct. They typically can't tolerate these unpleasant feelings (sadness, guilt, remorse, shame, etc.) and try to escape via more impulsive pleasure-seeking. That's how they become addicted.

It would be difficult to over-emphasize the importance of this principle, especially in a society that urges you to get it all now. Credit is easily obtained and bankruptcy available if you get in too deep. Sex before marriage is the norm. American business is reluctant to fund long-term research and development because boards of directors and stockholders are only looking at next quarter's profits. The country is trillions of dollars in debt for pork-barrel spending. Hit the tanning bed today and worry about the oncologist later. We're obsessed with the immediate gratification of our desires. We're not necessarily happy. **Yet a key to living a happy life is learning to defer gratification, to act responsibly, and work hard today for a better future**. Truly happy people even learn to enjoy working hard, doing a good job, and anticipating later rewards.

The Way of Wealth:

My practice is centrally located between three of the wealthiest communities in Alabama, and my clientele derives largely from these areas. They aren't coming to see me because they're happy. **Evidently simply having money doesn't guarantee happiness**, though, fortunately, it will buy you a lot of psychotherapy.

It's widely claimed that money won't buy you happiness, but behavior indicates that many (most?) people don't believe it. We all chase the Mighty Bucks sometimes, and some people are so obsessed in the pursuit of wealth that this clearly represents their chosen plan for happiness. So why doesn't it work?

The truth is that money in and of itself is worthless. You can't eat it, drink it, sleep on it, lie in it or drive it to work. You can only spend it, which means you use it to obtain other ways to be happy. **The way of wealth often boils down to either pleasure-seeking or power-seeking.** We've already seen the futility of pleasure-seeking and we'll look later to the problems of the way of power. The trouble in both is that they only get you what you want, and that doesn't make people happy. "Spoiled brats" get whatever they want and yet are notoriously unhappy people. They demand everything and appreciate nothing. They drive people away with their selfishness and are unloved by self or by others. **They get what they want, but not what they need.**

People use money to meet a surprising variety of psychological needs, with varying degrees of success. For example, many people base their self-esteem on money, as if one's worth as a human being could be measured in dollars. I must be a good person, they reason, because I'm such a wealthy one. While this logic is pretty specious and the value system superficial, this works well for a lot of people - until they go broke. The problem is that self-worth is intrinsic, something fundamental to a person's character. Wealth is extrinsic and depends on external factors unrelated to the person and often outside his control. Wealth often depends on luck, such as hitting the lottery, or being born into the right family. There's always somebody wealthier and therefore "better" than you. And there's always the possibility of losing your money. Thus, there never seems to be quite enough for you to relax and feel good about yourself. Many people lose their wealth through no fault of their own. Yet, if they have based their self-esteem on wealth and success, their self-esteem plummets when their bank account drops, even if the cause was totally out of their control. That's just not right.

For many people money is essentially a security blanket. They feel "safe" because they've saved up a certain amount of loot. But people who survived the Great Depression know how evanescent this kind of security can be. Stocks crashed and banks closed, factories shut down and well-established businesses went bankrupt. People went overnight from riches to rags and lost all control of their destinies. For people who grew up in those times, there isn't enough money in the world to make them feel safe. Better to trust in your own survival skills or earning potential than to place your security in a bank vault. As with self-esteem, security is a feeling inside yourself and can't truly be gotten in the exterior world. You can feel safe if you know that you are flexible, adaptable, and resourceful enough to get by, no matter what may occur. Here I am in a non-salaried job in a highly volatile and unpredictable industry (health care), yet I feel relatively secure. That's because I can and will do whatever I need to in order to survive. (I have, however, also paid off the mortgage, put money aside and married a woman with a relatively secure job. I feel secure in myself, but it doesn't hurt to hedge your bets a bit and be prudent with your money.)

I'm not arguing that wealth is evil, rich people are bad, or the accumulation of wealth is a mistake. I'm just saying it won't make you happy in and of itself. **In fact, many of the happiest rich people I know aren't happy so much because of the money as because of the way they make it.** They love being surgeons or trial lawyers or CEOs. I've met many highly achieving people for whom the fun was in playing the game. The money was a way of keeping score. I even met a very successful businessman who sold his company so he could start all over with a new one. He found he was bored being a high-powered CEO. What he liked was the excitement, hard work, even the fearful uncertainties of *becoming* rich and successful.

My first year in graduate school I lived on $200 a month. Now my income, combined with my wife's is fifty times as much. But I'm not fifty times happier. My standard of living has gone up a lot, but I was mostly happy then, and I'm mostly happy now. **You can be happy in a hovel or miserable in a mansion. It's not where you live, but how you live that matters.**

The Way of Power:

Closely akin to the way of pleasure, this method has to do with making you happy by acquiring the power to control others. The idea, of course, is to get what you want by making other people do what you want them to do. "Bring me a beer; sell 10,000 shares of GMC; fire that idiot; tow that barge, lift that bale." There's an infinite variety of commands that can result in your being happy, if you have the power to make them obeyed. In many cases, the way of power really boils down to the ways of pleasure and wealth, only with other people as our agents. For others, however, power is an end in itself. They aren't really interested in pleasure or wealth, in exercising power to get rich, get drunk, or whatever. They simply enjoy - - or rather, crave - - the feeling of satisfaction they derive from getting their way and making others do their bidding. It makes them feel strong, capable, adequate, even superior to dominate others. It builds their self-esteem. It is as if they say to themselves: "I must be better than you, because I'm more powerful." Here, we find a hint of the self-defeating nature of this way to find happiness. In the exercise of power, there's always a bit of hostility, and hostility means resentment.

If I have power over you, you are likely to be afraid of me and how I'll use my power. You may also respect me, or my authority, but you are not likely to have much affection for me. Power can gain your respect and your fear, but not your love or your loyalty. You'll resent me and you'll take every opportunity to resist my control, to defy, to rebel, hopefully to overthrow me. Actively and openly if you can, passive-aggressively if you can't, you'll rebel against me, try to assume my position of power and then use it to dominate me. And since you are angry and resentful, you'll try to hurt me.

It is a truism that "power corrupts." Benevolent despots tend to become simply malevolent despots. Power goes to your head, makes you feel superior to others, makes you think your way is the right way, just because you can get your way. Besides, as people resist your power, you feel threatened with its loss and therefore crack down harder on the resisters. The relationship between powerful and powerless is a hostile one, and it has a strong tendency to become downright sadistic. As George Orwell pointed out in *1984*, the ultimate test of power is the ability to hurt somebody. If I can hurt you with impunity, but you can't hurt me, then clearly, I have the more powerful position. To prove my power I simply do something to hurt you. Repeatedly. This makes me feel good because it reinforces my feeling of power. Thus, the way of power tends to degenerate into frank sadism, the gaining of pleasure by way of hurting others.

As with the other ways we've examined by which people seek happiness, the exercise of power isn't necessarily or inevitably evil or unsuccessful. It is a normal human desire and essential for the development of self-esteem to develop a certain level of mastery over one's environment and one's self. Witness the look of triumph on a toddler's face when he first climbs the stairs unaided. Remember the joy you felt when you mastered the bicycle, circling the neighborhood shakily, but without training wheels. This kind of power or mastery is an essential pre-condition for both self-esteem ("I'm OK because I can take care of myself") and a sense of personal security ("I feel safe because I can successfully cope with life's challenges.") Failure to learn how to like yourself and trust in your own abilities leads directly to the kind of emotional disturbance which lands people in the therapist's office. Research shows, for example, that depressed people are much more likely than others to have a pervasive feeling that they are out of control of their own lives. They are hopeless because they have no confidence in their own ability to make life worth living. Low self-esteem, on the other hand, is associated with most, if not all, emotional and interpersonal problems. It drives people into all kinds of self-destructive relationships and self-defeating behavior patterns. Promiscuous sexuality, for example, is often an attempt to gain approval and affection from others by a person who has no respect or affection for herself. Each encounter provides a brief "fix" but also ends up making the person feel cheap, unlovable, and "used." The only quick solution is another affair, restarting this addictive behavior cycle.

Having the power to do things well, to cope with life effectively and to relate to others does tend to make you feel happy and secure. But notice that we are talking here about power over yourself, and to some extent, over your environment. We are not talking about the power to control, and hurt, others. As we have seen, that way of Power won't necessarily lead to happiness for you or for others. I've seen people who scramble madly and back-stab viciously to get a little political power in their work. They barely have time to gloat over their success before they begin plotting their next move. They're never satisfied.

The Way of Success:

One of the world's great philosophers was a Southern comic with a vague ministerial connection by the name of "Brother Dave Gardner." In one of the best simple statements ever uttered about happiness, Brother Dave neatly pointed to the error in seeking happiness by way of success. "Success," said Brother Dave, "is getting what you want, but **happiness is wanting what you get.**" Spoiled brats and tyrants get what they want, yet never seem happy with it. True happiness, on the contrary, comes from a calm acceptance and appreciation of what you have.

As with the other ways we've examined, there's nothing inherently wrong with trying to be successful. Succeeding in our work builds self-esteem, and a certain amount of success is essential to put meat on the table. Succeeding in our marriage provides a happy, stable home for ourselves and our children. Success brings a thrill of triumph and joy that's good for our physical as well as our mental health. Failure, on the other hand, can be discouraging, even depressing (though it can also serve as a spur to even greater achievement later.)

Success is a good thing and worth pursuing. The mistake is in thinking that success: 1) makes you a good person, and 2) automatically makes you happy. Taking the second point first, a quick observation of the world around us is enough to document that many successful people simply aren't very happy. Successful people experience as much depression, suicide, divorce, alcoholism, and disease as do unsuccessful ones. Success in one area provides no immunity from failure in others, and this failure may lead to great unhappiness. Indeed, success often brings with it all sorts of troubles and cares that interfere with happiness: more responsibilities, more hassles, more insurance salesmen trying to share in your success. Often the cost of succeeding in one area of life is failure in another. How many marriages have failed because a workaholic spouse succeeded in business, but neglected his family? How often does becoming a success turn people into greedy, mean, selfish, dictatorial or emotionally distant people? Many people succeed professionally, while failing as persons. They and their families both end up unhappy. No one can be consistently successful in everything he undertakes. Does this mean it is impossible to be happy?

I'm currently seeing a pessimistic young lady who believes it is essential to her happiness and self-worth to be highly successful and who further believes that she is very unlikely to be a success. She's already unhappy and she hasn't even failed yet! She's bright, talented, attractive, and diligent and her grades are excellent. Yet she has no self-esteem, has no confidence in her future, and sees herself a failure. Unfortunately there is a self-fulfilling quality to her prediction of failure. She is less likely to succeed because she doesn't believe she can and she may therefore be less likely to "go for it" and do what is necessary to succeed. Fear of failure may itself be the greatest cause of failure.

As we've already implied, part of the difficulty with setting success as the key to your happiness has to do with the subjective definition of success. While there are some more-or-less objective and agreed-upon definitions, "Success" is defined differently by each of us. It depends on how you set your goals. Do you want to be successful in business, in marriage, or in art? If you are successful artistically you may be a commercial failure and vice-versa. Is a successful psychologist one who publishes many professional papers, one whose patients get better, or one who makes a lot of money doing therapy? How high you set your standards is also an individual choice and can determine whether you "succeed" or "fail" in your own mind. If you define financial success as making ten million dollars and you only make nine million, then you're a failure. For some runners a successful race is one in which they set a world record; for others success is just finishing standing up.

Another of my young patients has a swimming career which neatly parallels my own career in track: neither of us ever won a race. However I feel good about my running, while she feels worthless and defeated as a swimmer. Naturally, I tried to win every time I raced and would have loved to set records, make the Olympics, etc. I'm just not all that fast. But my goals were to make the team, to get in shape, to do my best, to improve my times, and to enjoy the comradeship of my teammates. Since I did all of that, I felt like a success. My patient's goal is to be the best, so she feels like a failure.

The subjectivity of the definition of success has profound implications for one's self-esteem or feeling of self-worth. Two athletes have identical performance records, yet one feels himself a success while the other sees herself a failure. Perhaps the problem here is an inappropriate definition or standard of "success," coupled with an inappropriate linking of success and self-esteem. Since there is no single objective standard, each of us gets to define success in his or her own terms. In a sense, we're all really racing against ourselves. So why set yourself an unrealistically high standard that guarantees you'll fail? Isn't it better to succeed at trying *my* best than to fail at being *the* best.

Further, it is inappropriate to link your self-esteem or sense of self-worth to success because self-esteem is intrinsic and success is extrinsic. Your value or worth as a human being has to do with your character, not your achievement. It is who you are, not what you've done. Self-worth is not measured in dollars (or, to the anorectic's dismay, pounds). Success, on the other hand, is extrinsic, having to do with the world outside us. It depends on all sorts of factors that have nothing to do with you as a person. Some ordinary people are fabulously successful out of pure dumb luck, while other creative and industrious folks end up failing due to bad-timing or other events beyond their control. Some successful people are real jerks, while some failures are wonderful human beings.

One of my favorite uncles made a fortune in real estate and, naturally, was proud of his success. Unfortunately, he did it in a town highly dependent on oil money. When the Arabs dumped oil on the market in '83, the town dried up and you literally couldn't give away real estate. My uncle's business declined dramatically and he fell into a deep depression. Apparently his self-esteem was based largely on his success in business. Now he saw himself as a failure and therefore a worthless person. I felt he was mistaken for two reasons. Firstly, OPEC's move caught everybody napping. His failure to anticipate this event was no indication of a lack of business acumen. Further, he had in fact protected his family as best he could from just such a reversal, saving money, etc. Secondly, to my way of thinking, my uncle was a great guy before he struck it rich and was still a great guy after his reversal of fortunes. I was proud of his accomplishments and sorry for his loss, but neither one changed how I saw him as a person.

The Way of Fame:
This way of seeking happiness falls into the group of wealth, power, success, and pleasure. All depend on obtaining something in the outside world. There are many people who long for glory and believe that becoming well-known will make them happy. A brief glance at the entertainment tabloids ought to dissuade them, yet people persist in believing that fame brings happiness. If this were true, why are the rates of drug abuse, divorce, infidelity, and suicide so high in the music and movie businesses? Likewise, why can't royalty make happy marriages and why do they struggle so to elude the paparozzi? You can achieve instant world-wide fame by climbing up a tower and picking off passers-by with a high-powered rifle. Don't count on it making you happy, though. More

likely you'll end up dead or, at best, rotting away in prison.

Fame and the other strategies we've examined so far all fail to provide happiness in the long run because all depend on stimulation from external sources. They provide a temporary "fix," a jolt of pleasure of excitement or triumph. They do not provide true happiness, which comes from within. Or they provide a temporary ego boost, but not true and lasting self-esteem, which, by definition, comes only from yourself. You're constantly dependent on this outside source of "happiness" and can never rest secure in your own ability to make yourself happy. You can, of course, tell yourself, "I must be a good and valuable person because I'm so famous (rich, powerful, successful, etc.)" and thereby bolster your own self esteem. But you can even more easily say, "I'm a good person because I am who I am; I don't need to be famous to be myself." Then you needn't worry about fame.

What makes you famous may make you happy, or it may not. Fame itself is a fairly cheap commodity and easy to obtain, especially if you're willing to sacrifice your good judgement or good taste. But fame in and of itself isn't worth much. It also tends to be fleeting, as Andy Warhol pointed out. It does pump the old ego a bit to read your name in print, see yourself interviewed on TV, or, I would imagine, to see your name go up in theater lights. It feels good to be noticed, paid attention to, considered noteworthy. Nonetheless, the way of fame is hardly an effective long-term strategy for achieving happiness. Again, the fundamental error is in thinking that something *out there* is going to make you happy, instead of learning to make yourself happy, out there.

The Way of Narcissism:

In ancient Greek mythology, Narcissus was said to be an astonishingly handsome young man. He was so beautiful that everyone who saw him fell in love with him. In fact, Narcissus happened to see his image reflected in a pool of water and he fell in love with himself! A nymph named Echo also fell in love with him, but Narcissus was so busy adoring his own image that her song of love fell on deaf ears. Poor Echo heard only the reflection of her own voice. The myth of Narcissus and Echo neatly summarizes not only the psychological process now known as narcissism, but what life is like for the people involved with narcissistic persons.

A positive self-image seems to be more or less essential to the maintenance of good mental health. Unfortunately we all have personal attributes that aren't so positive, making self-esteem and self-love a bit of a tricky business. It is a rare individual who can truly see himself exactly as he really is without suffering some blow to the ego and some loss of self-esteem. Thus, we all develop what psychology calls "defense mechanisms" to protect ourselves from the unpleasant realities of our lives, our deeds, and our selves. For example, we insulate ourselves from the pain of failure by "rationalizing" that we really didn't want to win and wouldn't have enjoyed our success anyway. Or perhaps we deal with a tragic loss at a purely intellectual level and thereby avoid a painful period of mourning. Rationalization and intellectualization are normal defense mechanisms we all use regularly, and they do help us cope with the "slings and arrows of outrageous fortune." Likewise, repression, suppression, denial, projection, and other defense mechanisms are normal and healthy.

But all defense mechanisms inevitably involve to some degree or another, an element of the denial of reality. Thus, they can become pathological and problematical. Paranoids, for example, over-utilize the defense mechanism of **Projection**. They see the world as hostile to them and out to get them. But the truth is that they are merely projecting their own anger, which they cannot accept, onto others. Paranoids are the most hostile people around. Narcissism is another defense mechanism which can get quite out of hand and become terribly destructive.

The essence of narcissism is to protect oneself from a feeling of inferiority by adopting instead a posture of superiority. Something happens, typically in the earliest years of life, ages three to five, that constitutes a near-mortal blow to the child's self-esteem. It may be rejection by one's peers, abuse, or humiliation by a parent, or perhaps a physical deformity. Whatever it is, this "narcissistic injury" is such a blow to the developing ego that it cannot be tolerated. To the child it is a clear indication that he is inadequate, inferior, unacceptable, or unlovable. He is not good enough and cannot hold himself in high esteem. The pain of this injury is unendurable.

Here's where the defense mechanism of narcissism kicks in. The child, unable to tolerate a fear of inferiority, decides instead that it is all a mistake. He is, in fact, superior to others. The negative view of himself is discarded and replaced with a positive one, which is then presented to the world. Like Narcissus, the budding narcissist "falls in love" with his beautiful new image and seeks to be adored by others as well. This will confirm the accuracy of the grand new image.

Within limits, a little narcissism is normal and healthy, if not particularly endearing. It is a defense mechanism used occasionally by most bright, beautiful, and talented people. In fact, it is only available to such persons, since an obviously stupid, ugly, incompetent person will simply appear ludicrous if he acts superior. But narcissism can become the central, organizing dynamic of a person's character and can dominate his life. When this happens it is called a "narcissistic personality disorder," and it can be quite pathological. Indeed, its most extreme and malignant form is sociopathy, the vicious, even criminal exploitation of others.

The narcissist rejects a negative, but to some extent accurate self-image and replaces it with a grand and glorious one. He creates and endorses a "grandiose false self," a facade of superiority, which he then tries to sell to the world. Narcissists build themselves up shamelessly, bragging on or even fabricating great triumphs and achievements. Simultaneously they try to elevate themselves by criticizing, mocking, or denigrating others. They demand excessive admiration, mingle only with other high-status people, and expect special privileges because of their superiority. They are inveterate name-droppers. They have a sense of entitlement and may be arrogant and exploitative to others. Anything which questions, criticizes, or tarnishes this image will be experienced by the narcissist as a repetition of the original narcissist injury and will send him into a rage. Narcissists do not take criticism well, since any flaw or weakness in the elegant facade they have constructed threatens to send the whole image crumbling into ruins. The narcissist knows everything and he is *always* right.

As an overall strategy for achieving happiness in life, narcissism is a flop. Narcissists are often quite charming and their achievements and erudition impressive. But their self-absorption, lack of empathy, disregard for others, vanity, sheer arrogance, and angry outbursts are far from endearing. They usually experience great difficulty maintaining long-term intimate relationships. Because they do not have genuine self-love, their ability to love others is greatly impaired. That's one reason, "it's lonely at the top." Narcissists are emotionally locked in at the age they adopted this mechanism, namely three or four. Thus, they often have a boyish charm and playfulness which are highly attractive. But they also go into rages, which are not. Rage is not an adult emotion, but rather that of a toddler. In adults it is ugly, frightening, and unacceptable.

Narcissism is tiring, as the image must be continually polished and enhanced. You're only as good as your latest triumph, so constant and uninterrupted success is a must. Being a know-it-all in our current information explosion takes a lot of work. As age begins to take its toll on the beautiful image, diet, work-outs, and plastic surgery take over your life. Your competitors are nipping at your heels.

Even as a defense mechanism, narcissism ultimately fails because it involves a fundamental denial of reality. Narcissists appear to have vastly inflated egos. In truth they have no real ego at all. Instead they have replaced it with a false self. The narcissist may be fabulously successful and may convince all the world he is as wonderful as he purports to be. But he can never believe it himself, because he knows it is all a sham, a facade, a false image he has constructed for himself. Beneath the air of superiority the terrible fear of inadequacy is always there, constantly threatening to expose and humiliate him. Self-esteem and peace of mind continue to elude him. He's never truly happy with himself.

Spouses of narcissistic persons invariably recognize this insecurity and fear of inadequacy in their mates. They may even find it somewhat appealing, as it may be the only genuine, innocent and vulnerable emotion evident in their spouse. Many women marry narcissistic men because they unconsciously want to mother the hurt child they perceive behind the admittedly impressive facade. Unfortunately their attempts to nurture and reassure their husbands are often met with hostility and contempt, as the narcissist sees in them an implied but unacceptable criticism. They can admit no fear, accept no weakness, and therefore receive no love. Their lack of true self-love, both keeps them from loving and also from feeling loved.

As one might expect, narcissism is often the motive underlying the pursuit of wealth, success, or fame. These are sought not for themselves but because they attest to the glory of the seeker, bolstering the narcissistic self-image. Narcissism can, by the way, be quite selective, limited only to those areas of life considered by the individual to be of importance. Thus, one may seek to be adored for physical beauty while another holds this in disdain and indeed is content to be frumpy and disheveled... so long as he is admired for his superior knowledge, great wit, and exquisite taste in wines.

I have used the masculine pronoun in this discussion because narcissism is considerably more common in males, just as "borderline personality" is in females. Hence the term "fragile male ego." The way of "machismo" might be considered a sub-type of narcissism which emphasizes superior strength and courage. It might also be noted that narcissistic males and borderline females are very alike in some ways: both tend to bounce from one extreme to another, to express excessive levels of emotion, and to swing from extremes of adoration to extremes of denigration (whether of self or others). Both are utterly self-absorbed. Borderlines and narcissists, by the way, find each other quite irresistible, but they get along about as well as lions and gazelles. Borderlines and narcissists share a common love object– the narcissist. The borderline personality lacks a coherent sense of self, while the narcissistic personality seems to have an excess of ego. The borderline seems to sense she can gain an identity through her linkage to the narcissist. She also finds him strong and capable, appealing to her dependency needs. The narcissist finds it flattering to be adored and idealized by the borderline. Besides, she is obviously a highly discerning person, since she likes him. Unfortunately, both have serious problems, and their union only compounds them.

Narcissism is a treatable problem unless the individual is so malignant as to be truly sociopathic. The main obstacle to overcome is to get the patient to accept the fact he needs help, which of course is utterly contrary to the central dynamic of his life. Most of the narcissistic patients I have seen have been dragged in resentfully by despairing wives, referred under court order, or are otherwise under the gun and facing ejection from school, disbarment, divorce or public exposure. Surprisingly, they are often amazed and greatly relieved to find their secret inner life so readily perceived and understood. They quickly recognize themselves in the story of Narcissus and not infrequently cry softly to be finally understood, accepted and offered an end to their struggle.

The way out of narcissism is simple to describe, but difficult to accomplish. It is to reject both extremes, both the narcissistic grandiosity and the terrible fear of inadequacy. It is to accept that you are neither superior to nor inferior to the rest of humanity. Then decide that you are "okay," and that is "good enough." **"Good enough" is not the ideal, but it is, by definition, good enough. And it is a realistic and sustainable self-image that one can be happy with for a lifetime.**

So far we've dealt with approaches to finding happiness that involve getting something from the world, be it pleasure, wealth, power, success, or fame. They are all relatively unsophisticated, self-serving, and ineffective. They are addictive but ultimately unsatisfying. These ways to happiness all involve a focus on the Self, on doing things to make yourself feel good, even at the expense of others. What, then, of the opposite approach, of making yourself happy by giving something to the world? We turn now for an examination of ways to happiness that involve serving others, or serving a cause rather than self. These might be said to be Other-focused strategies, because they are directed toward doing something for somebody else, albeit in hopes of making one's self happy in the long run.

Chapter Three. Other-Focused Strategies for Happiness
The Way of Service:

There are numerous variations on this strategy, but all involve trying to obtain happiness by doing things for other people. This may involve taking care of others, rescuing distressed souls, ministering to the sick or simply doing things to please other people. In some way you serve others and receive in return their love, approval, or gratitude. Or you simply receive the joy of giving. This strategy shows considerably more promise than the ones we've been looking at. It isn't so likely to be addictive. This is a more sophisticated strategy that recognizes the value of other people and the enlightened self-interest of making others happy. Alfred Adler taught that neurotics are lacking in "social interest" and are too self-absorbed. If he was right (and he certainly had a point, at least) people who adopt this strategy should have a higher probability of being mentally healthy and happy. However, it is not without its potential drawbacks and pitfalls. Let's look more closely at these various approaches and their relative advantages and disadvantages.

In our time Mother Theresa best exemplifies a life spent ministering to the needs of others. (It should be noted that in her view she was serving God, not just other human beings. Thus, Mother Theresa also represents the way of spirituality, to be discussed below). She was the caretaker par excellence, never marrying and living in absolute poverty. She gave away her wealth and sought only to succeed in helping the poor. She gained fame, without seeking it, and used it to advance the causes of peace and charity. She had only the power of her moral force and she used it to persuade the world's leaders to advance the common good. She was celibate and to my knowledge, had no vices. Yet, Mother Theresa may have been the best-loved person in the world and by all accounts one of the happiest. Mother Theresa's life clearly indicates that caretaking, or ministering to the needs of others, can make you happy. On a scale far less grand, my father grew up next door to a woman who devoted her entire life to caring for a profoundly retarded and disabled daughter. Far from becoming embittered or ever seeing herself as a martyr, this good woman felt happy and fulfilled, ever blessed by her lot in life. She wasn't rich, famous, powerful or successful, yet she found happiness by devoting herself to another's care.

Why does this strategy work? Taking care of others focuses your attention not on yourself but on the other. Self-absorption, egotism and narcissism are therefore avoided. Since the other is in need of care, he is presumably less fortunate than you. Thus, service to others tends to remind you of your own good fortune and help you appreciate what you have. Caretakers give of their time, their energy, their material goods, and themselves. Thus, they experience the joy of giving. They have good reasons to feel good about themselves and what they do. They lead meaningful, valuable, productive lives. They contribute to society instead of taking from it. Thus, they tend to be held in high esteem by others as well as by themselves.

There is no doubt that a life of service to others can be enormously rewarding and produce a lot of happiness. Nonetheless, it does have its disadvantages. Service to others can be extremely taxing in terms of your time, your energy, and often your patience. Service professions typically don't pay very well, though there are exceptions. Medicine, for example, has been reasonably lucrative, at least until recently. More typically, nursing, teaching, and child care pay far less. (Psychology is in-between and currently headed down-scale.) Volunteer service, by definition, doesn't pay at all. Working conditions aren't necessarily so great, either. Mother Theresa's vocation took her to the poorest, dirtiest slums of Calcutta and surrounded her with unwashed, diseased, and desperately needy people. You can surely make yourself happy by serving others, but you'll definitely earn your happiness.

We've been focusing up to now on people who devote their whole lives to serving others, either professionally or as volunteers. However, there's a sense in which all or at least most jobs have an element of service to them. A waitress serves you a meal, a mechanic services your car, and your TV is repaired by a "serviceman." **Thus, most people can**

experience some of the happiness that comes from a life of service, whatever their career.
This isn't naive or wishful thinking, either. If my toilets are blocked and flooding the house, I feel very much taken care of by the plumber who fixed them. And I don't need a Sister of Charity unless she's handy with a monkey wrench. Volunteer work, of course is also open to anyone. If one adopts the way of service, one must be careful about how and where the service is rendered. Caretaker relationships in marriage, for example, can be quite problematical (as we'll see again, later). Caretaker marriages tend to become unbalanced in terms of power and can lead to destructive behavior patterns. The caretaker may feel trapped or used by the dependent spouse and may develop strong resentments. Meanwhile, the one taken care of may resent the control inevitably exercised by the caretaker. Taking care of an alcoholic spouse may help you to feel needed, but it also enables the alcoholic to go on drinking. All marriages have at least temporary elements of caretaking, but as a permanent basis for a marriage, caretaking and dependency lead to more unhappiness than the contrary.

How well the way of service works depends in large measure on the motivation and expectations of the particular individual. The joy of giving is only available to those who give with an open heart. If you're in a service profession, it's OK to expect compensation for your work. However, if remuneration is your only motive, then you're actually operating more from the way of wealth, not that of service. Likewise, it's fine to expect some appreciation for your efforts, but demanding recognition and honors is the way of fame, not service. Serving others makes you happy if you do it for love of them (or of God) and because it feels good to do it. It's likely not to make you happy if you serve others thinking they will love you for it. In fact, it's likely to backfire and lead to unhappiness. Here's how:

It's not possible to make others love you; that's under their control, not yours. If you take care of me and do things for me I may love what you do but still not like *you* much at all. In fact, I may actually lose affection and respect for you, seeing you as a sycophant, people-pleaser, or door mat. Many people truly believe they can make others love them. "If I do this for you, then you *must* love me. I can make it happen." They are shocked when they fail to get love in return. Similarly, they believe others *must* be grateful for these services, even if the services were never requested or even desired. Again, they end up disappointed and upset. At this point, they often get angry with the other person. "How dare you not love me?" they say in effect.

The other person is generally taken aback. "I never agreed to love you," he might say. "Further, I never asked you to do those things for me." It is as if the caretaker is trying to strike a bargain with the rest of the world, but doing it unilaterally, without consulting them or securing their agreement. Then she gets angry when the other fails to keep his end of a contract he didn't even know existed. This is a behavior pattern seen in its most extreme in persons with "borderline personality disorder." These people tend to see the world as all black or all white and see others as all bad or all good. They flip unpredictably from one side to the other but can't maintain a middle position. They try desperately to please and to win love, then furiously reject the other if they don't get love just the way they want it. Understandably, they have extreme difficulty maintaining long-term relationships and often end up feeling empty, lonely, and unloved.

Excessive, inappropriate caretaking often develops in children of alcoholics, as we will see again later. These children grow up taking care of the alcoholic parent, instead of the reverse. Whatever "love" they get from the parent is tied to this caretaking. Thus, they learn that one must earn love by taking care of and trying to please others, and they carry this behavior pattern into other relationships. Adult children of alcoholics tend to marry people who need to be taken care of (alcoholics, for example) and set up inappropriate "co-dependent" relationships.

People-Pleasing:

Taking care of others in order to earn their love, gratitude and approval easily degenerates into simple people-pleasing. Many people believe that if they do whatever others want in order to please them, they will receive in return the other's love and approval. This will make them happy. It turns out, however, that people-pleasing is not so easy and usually doesn't work very well. As we noted earlier, there are some people out there who simply aren't pleased by anything or anybody. Nothing you can do will earn their approval. If you act (or look) one way there's one set of folks who won't approve, but switch to another and a whole new group disapproves of you. You can't please all the people all the time, even if you try to change yourself to accommodate them. You can also exhaust yourself trying.

Further, if you do change yourself to please others, you may find that you come across as a phony (understandably enough) or lacking in character and integrity. You may be seen as a brown-noser, butt-kisser, yes-man, or other form of sycophant and therefore lose people's approval. You may lose self-respect as well, and this will certainly lead to more unhappiness. **What people really want is to be loved, accepted, and approved of as they are. You can't get this by becoming somebody else.** Even if people were pleased by whom you pretended to be or actually came to be, you still wouldn't feel approved for your own true self. And in trying to please others, you're in real danger of losing track of who you truly are. If you act in ways you yourself disapprove of, you lose integrity. If you continually try to

-63-

please others, you fail to please yourself. I've met people who'd spent so many years trying to please others that they no longer knew what they liked, valued or believed in themselves. They couldn't choose a restaurant because they no longer knew what kind of food they preferred!

People who engage in excessive people-pleasing are actually hard to get along with at times. They won't tell you what they really want to do because they're afraid to displease you. Yet later they may express disappointment or regret about your choice. You look like the bad guy, even though you'd have happily accommodated their wishes. You end up being responsible for all decision-making. In effect, you end up being responsible for the other person's happiness. Meanwhile, the people-pleaser may be trying so hard that he becomes annoyingly obsequious. What would really please you is for the other to make a choice or perhaps to go away and leave you alone, but how do you say this to someone who strives so earnestly to please?

For some people-pleasers their efforts are focused not on people in general, but on one specific individual. If only x will approve of them, then they can approve of themselves and be happy. In my experience, though, this individual is invariably someone who approves of no-one (save possibly himself). This may be a complaining wife, a demanding boss, or a spoiled child, but typically the people-pleaser has selected someone who is impossible to please. Most commonly it is a critical, demanding, perfectionistic parent.

A businessman sought my help because he was depressed and suffered from low self-esteem. The son of a highly critical, disapproving father, he had struggled all his life to win the old man's approval. Nothing was ever good enough to please his Dad. If you made the A honor roll, Dad demanded to know why it wasn't straight A's. Scoring a touchdown brought Dad's demand for two. This man's mission in life came to be the earning of his father's approval. Only then could he approve of himself. After college he went to work for the company his father had built, owned, and controlled. Again, nothing pleased his Dad. If he sold a million-dollar contract, it should have been two. On he labored, to no avail. Finally, when he was forty his father called him in and announced he was retiring from the company. Naturally, he wanted to leave his business in the best possible hands, he said, since he'd put his whole life into it. Much to the son's amazement, his father then made him the CEO and gave the business to him! More amazingly, he was doing this not just because he loved his son, (which was the first time in forty years he'd told him so), but because the son was the best businessman he'd ever seen– including himself. Predictably, my patient was overwhelmed, having finally achieved his life-long ambition of receiving his father's approval. "So why are you here to see me?" I asked. Because, he said, his father's approval, while enormously gratifying, wasn't enough; he still didn't really approve of himself. "Unfortunately," I replied, "you can't get self-esteem from somebody else. That's why it's called SELF-esteem. You must provide it for yourself." He'd already begun to figure that out.

People-pleasers are always stunned to hear this, but the truth is that at heart their behavior is manipulative. They are trying to manipulate, coax, con people into liking and approving of them. And people simply don't like being manipulated. There's an inherent, if subtle, element of deceitfulness and control. The inveterate people-pleaser isn't acting altruistically, in the interest of the other person; he's trying to get what HE needs. He does it under the guise of serving others, but people-pleasing is often more self-serving– and others may resent it.

That the people-pleaser is actually interested primarily in herself is evident in one of the ways this strategy backfires: people-pleasers are often noted to be highly and anxiously *self-conscious*. People-pleasers enter a social situation with one primary, underlying concern: Will these people like me? They aren't really interested in getting to know anybody, just in people getting to know and like *them*. Their constant concern is with how they look, how they are coming across, what kind of feedback they are getting from others, whether or not they are liked. They aren't paying attention to the other person, but to themselves. They truly are what the phrase implies, namely *conscious of themselves*. This becomes a substantial barrier to connecting with the other person. You can't really pay attention to anyone else when your mind is preoccupied with yourself, and it shows. People-pleasers are surprised to hear themselves described as preoccupied, distracted, or just plain stuck-up. But that's how they come across. It's as if they enter every room with the vague suspicion there's a booger sticking out of one nostril. They are so taken with surreptitious attempts to remove it that they are totally distracted. This strikes others as rude and drives away would-be friends. The people-pleaser thus brings on the very happening she fears most, rejection. I advise my people-pleasing, self-conscious patients to forget about themselves in social situations and pay attention to the other people there. Who do *you* like? What is interesting to me about this other person and what she is saying? If the other person doesn't like you, that's *his* problem, and you'll likely find out soon enough.

There are other ways the people-pleaser sabotages himself socially just because he is so interested in being liked and so fearful of rejection. These are people who typically do not like themselves very well. This being the case, they naturally assume a new acquaintance won't like them either. So when they meet new people, they keep their guard up, revealing little about themselves or trying to create a false, but likeable impression. This is a defense mechanism, but one which works by distancing yourself from the other.

It works, too. The other person feels himself pushed away and decides you don't want to be friends. So he leaves, leaving you to experience the very rejection you feared. And you made it happen yourself.

A particularly pernicious form of people-pleasing that has mushroomed enormously over the past few decades constitutes another way to happiness in and of itself. It is popularly called: Living for Your Children.

Living for Your Children:

We live in an era when children no longer seek the approval of their parents. Instead, we've reversed the natural and well-proven wisdom of centuries and adopted a system in which parents live for and seek to please their children. Parents sacrifice themselves, slave away for years, and thoroughly disrupt their family life to provide for their children a better life than they had as kids. It's no longer "a chicken in every pot," but "a TV, VCR, and video game machine in every kid's room." Whoops, forgot to mention a telephone. We shower our kids with the best of everything and labor mightily to keep them up with the Jones' kids. Even while running track, I got my shoes at the discount place and put cardboard liners in them to stretch their lifetime. My kids wear name-brand running shoes, though they wouldn't run if you whipped them. We live in the era of the child-focused family, the modern replacement to the parent-focused family. We live for our children and seek only to make them happy. In my opinion, this doesn't work for them or for us, and it represents a real perversion of proper family structure. Let's look at this way more closely.

The modern idea of family life is that it is centered around child-rearing, and that the goal of parenting is to make our children happy and full of self-esteem. It's an idea strongly fostered and encouraged by social scientists and mental health professionals like me and has been adopted whole-heartedly and with little questioning both by our educational establishment and by our culture at large. Thus, many modern American adults essentially devote their lives to making their children happy, assuming that this will make them happy also. What has been the result? I would argue that the first result has been to raise a whole lot of spoiled, rebellious, lazy, narcissistic children. We have convinced our children that the world revolves around them– because in *our* world, it does. They agree that it is our job to make them happy, and if they aren't happy, it is our fault. They feel entitled to all sorts of special privileges and see their parents' primary mission as providing them. They do not see that they have any responsibility in the matter, and many of them take none. They don't see that they owe the family anything for taking care of them and their needs. Thus, they squawk and protest when asked to do even the lightest chores around the house, yet think nothing of demanding they be taken to the mall on a whim, chauffeured to baseball, ballet, or laser tag, given unlimited funds for fun. At the same time, they have little appreciation for these things, having gotten them through no expenditure of their own in terms of time, effort, or money, and they often show little gratitude for their parents' efforts. I am speaking in generalities and describing only the worst of the younger generation. I am aware that there also exist responsible, considerate, well-mannered children, just as there are also responsible parents with good common sense when it comes to child-rearing. Still, it looks to me as if we've increased the ratio of poorly raised to well raised kids.

When it comes time for these pampered and indulged children to take responsibility for their own lives, their own happiness, their own bills, many of them are, predictably enough, utterly unprepared to shoulder the burden. Maturity, responsibility, and independence are not gained on the day you turn eighteen, suddenly and without gradual preparation and planning. Granted, it isn't easy to get started on a real career in today's economy, but it still seems a telling statistic that something like forty per cent of America's twenty-five year- olds are still living at home and dependent financially on their parents. **In my opinion, the goal of parenting is to raise an independent, self-reliant, responsible, loving, and more-or-less happy adult.** By this standard, the modern parental style of living for your children is bound to be a failure. The result is unhappy, dependent, demanding, self-centered, irresponsible people.

Well, what then of the self-esteem angle? Maybe these young adults aren't self-reliant, but aren't they at least on good terms with their own egos? From what I see, the answer would have to be no. As we've seen elsewhere in this work, you can't make somebody else feel good about himself. **Self-esteem is just what it says; it must come from yourself.** And we're not giving our kids self-esteem. If anything we may be depriving them of opportunities to get it. Kids aren't dumb, just uneducated. When they enter a school art show and find themselves receiving a ribbon that says "Participant," just like all the other kids, they rightly throw it away as something of no value. A contest with no winners is no contest at all. In a sense, all the entrants are as equally losers. This does nothing to build self-esteem. Likewise, when all the little league players take home a trophy, only the youngest are fooled into thinking they've accomplished anything worthy of pride. Again, what is actually achieved is the devaluing of the real champion's accomplishment and trophy. Helping a child to feel good about himself for having tried, even if he has failed, is a legitimate way to build self-esteem based on reality. Eliminating the very concept of failure, telling all children they are winners in all areas, simply sets them up for devastating blows to their self-esteem when they enter the real world, where failure is a fact of life. You can give your child a start towards self-esteem by loving her as unconditionally as you can and teaching her as much as you can about how to live effectively. From that point, however, she's on her own.

How well does living for your children work as a strategy for the parent who adopts it? In many ways, not much better, though again, it depends on just what you mean by this way of living. Does it make you happy in the short run to see your children happy? Sure it does, and there's nothing wrong with doing things to make them happy, to have fun with them, to teach them that life is also about play. But if that's all you do, you're likely to end up with irresponsible adult children like those we described above. That's unlikely to make them or you happy. Many parents expect their kids to end up making *them* happy, as if a bargain had been struck: I'll make you happy now, and you'll turn out to be a happy, healthy, responsible, loving adult who will shower me with lovely grandchildren and take care of me in my old age. Boy, are a lot of these parents going to be disappointed! Their kids will not appreciate what their parents have done, because they've been taught to expect it. They won't feel obligated to help out the old folks because they've been on the take all their lives. Many of these adult children will continue to use their parents, sponge off of them, dump the grandkids on them for free day care, then ignore and neglect them when they are in need. As with other forms of people-pleasing, living for your children is a unilateral bargain which is often left unfulfilled.

It is particularly a problem for mothers who have devoted their entire adult lives to taking care of their kids and making them happy. Many of these women are extraordinarily good at child-rearing and have relatively little else in their lives. They forego careers and hobbies for their kids. They derive their total self-esteem and meaning in life from mothering. Their self-image is entirely wrapped up in being a mother. This is fine while the kids are little, but what happens when they grow up? Poor old Mom is left with no role, no purpose in life, no basis for self-esteem. She has lived for her children and now may have nothing to live for. This is the so-called Empty Nest Syndrome. If her kids turn out like those we've been discussing, she may be bitterly disappointed, even angry or depressed. And if she's lost touch of Dad in her excessive devotion to Junior and sibs, she may have nowhere to turn to for consolation. Some mothers try to solve the problem by continuing to parent kids who don't need it, but this simply delays the inevitable, while encouraging irresponsibility in the young adult children. Some find other people in need of parenting, or perhaps use their grandchildren. None of these is an ideal solution, though they can work for some people, at least temporarily.

Besides the "empty nest syndrome" with its lonely, unfulfilled Moms, there are other ways that living for your children can go wrong. One is the Leaving Home scenario described elsewhere in this work. Here the parents try to continue in the parenting phase of their marriage past the time when the kids should be on their own. The child obliges by needing more parenting, either by being irresponsible, or by developing a mental illness, drug problem, or getting into trouble with the law. The result is a young adult who sacrifices herself to maintain the family structure and a set of frazzled, confused, and exhausted parents. In the long run, nobody prospers. I've seen a number of these troubled families, sometimes with "children" in their forties. Fortunately, they usually do quite well if you can convince them to turn the young adult offspring loose and insist they be responsible for themselves. Then the parents can turn to each other or to other ways to focus their attention and energy.

Some parents seem to be living for their children by becoming overly focused on and involved in the kids' activities and interests. These are the soccer moms who never miss a game or practice, cry to the coach about their little darlings' failure to get enough playing time, and yell exuberantly on every play despite a limited understanding of the game. These are the dads who demand perfection from their junior athletes, scream at the umpires, and revel in the accomplishments of their ballplayers. It's as if these parents have no life of their own, but live off the reflected glory of their progeny. They blame themselves if the kids don't win the championship, but they also take the credit if they do. "That's my boy" can easily become "I'm a great guy because my son scored the winning touchdown." Besides being an exercise in self-deception, this approach to parenting deprives the child of a life of his own and robs him of his achievements. It may also rob him of the joy of playing the game for its own sake. One day at the track I saw a man with two sons, aged about six and eight. He was running them up and down the bleachers, demanding they run laps, and slamming them repeatedly into a tackling dummy. He was obviously training them to be football stars and was doing it quite loudly, screaming at them to go faster and work harder. Poor kids– the best they can hope for is to be great players-- who hate the game. Dad, of course, had obviously not had a great football career himself, which was why he was trying to live through his kids. But your kids' glory is not your glory, and you can't obtain through them what you failed to accomplish on your own. All you can do is steal from them their own joy and sense of accomplishment.

Some parents try to continue to live through their children by taking over ownership and control of the grandchildren. In some cases this is necessary, because the young parents are incapable of parenting, usually because they are still children themselves. But in other cases, instead of helping their children raise the grandkids, parents co-opt this role for themselves. In so doing, they undercut the authority of the true parents, thereby virtually assuring that the grandchildren will grow up to be undisciplined and out of control.

There are also healthier ways of living at least partially for one's children. During their early childhood, for example, it is almost essential and unavoidable that the children will be the major focus of your time and energy. When our kids were little, we practically never socialized with adult friends and had whole weekends where we both ended up exhausted, yet accomplished nothing but taking care of the baby. Yet, even in their kids' younger years, parents are well advised to take time for themselves, as individuals and as a couple. Hang onto a sense of yourself as a person distinct from your role as parent. Have a life of your own to refresh and invigorate you and to which you can return as the kids grow up. Married couples should strive to hang onto their relationship as well, and not just as parents, but as husband and wife, man and woman. I advise at least one three-day weekend a year away from the kids, rediscovering each other.

Beyond this, most older people continue to see their children and grandchildren as a central focus of their lives and even as the primary source of meaning for them. Having descendants and heirs provides a sense of the continuity of life over the generations, a purpose for one's efforts and a way to live on past death. As most people become more elderly, they find that family has become the most meaningful and important thing in their lives. I have no quarrel with that. Yet, even where this is the case, healthy senior citizens have other interests, other friends, other ways to make themselves happy. They don't live exclusively for and through their children. Elderly couples often rediscover each other, and their relationship may be better than ever as they have time and the financial resources to travel together, visit old friends, and simply enjoy each others' company.

Martyrdom:

Getting back to the Way of Service, or of living for others, the ultimate in the way of service is the **Martyr**, who not only takes care of others but sacrifices his or her own life for others. As a one-shot strategy martyrdom shows promise because you can die happily, knowing you've given your life in a good cause, to someone you love. As a career strategy, however, it's severely limited. Unless you believe in reincarnation, you only have one life to give. Being a bit less literal-minded, many people do try to be happy by sacrificing themselves in smaller, less fatal ways. In a sense, all caretaking or service to others involves some degree of self-sacrifice, but this does not make one a martyr, as I am using the term here. Again, motivation and expectation determines the effectiveness and appropriateness of this strategy for happiness.

The "martyr" I'm thinking of here is an individual who does indeed chronically sacrifice his own will and desires for those of others, but who does so expecting sainthood in return. The sacrifice is made openly, even dramatically, but always with a "poor-me" sort of attitude. There's a clear message indicating how noble, long-suffering, down-trodden, and hard-working the martyr is. Others are expected to admire the martyr and to feel grateful for the sacrifice (whether it was requested or not.) In fact, they're also expected to feel at least a little guilty. The martyr feels sorry for herself and you're supposed to feel sorry too, which is why this kind of martyrdom wears thin pretty quickly.

Martyrs usually end up with everybody annoyed or angry with them. People get tired of the martyr's self-pity and wearied nobility. They may even offer to help speed up the martyrdom process by demanding more sacrifices . Please note that I'm not talking here of people who freely and generously devote themselves to the care of others. Such people don't see themselves as martyrs and don't come across as described above. They don't expect to be beatified or praised and they are content and happy. To them, the caretaking is its own reward.

Rescuing (and the Cycle of Abuse):

A final inappropriate, ineffective and potentially disastrous form of service to others is that of **Rescuing.** People who go around saving others are called "rescuers" or, sometimes, "wet puppy collectors." They can't resist riding to the rescue of a lost soul or pulling a poor, scared waif in from the storm. The payoffs are the victim's gratitude or love, the admiration of others, and the enhancement of one's self-worth that comes from putting one's self out, perhaps even into harm's way, for another. The downside is the potential costs involved. I once heard a whimper at my door, on a dark and stormy night (sorry). My German shepherd and I went to the door to find a cute, but sad and sickly cocker spaniel puppy. I didn't need another dog, but I couldn't let him die of exposure, so I took the shivering pup in, dried him, and fed him. He ended up costing me a couple of hundred dollars in veterinary bills before I gave him away. Such is the lot of wet puppy collectors– and the two-legged variety can be even more expensive.

Any decent fellow will naturally rush to the rescue of a damsel in distress. She will feel grateful and he will rightly consider himself a noble gentleman indeed. Rescuing, however, is not a sound basis for a long-term relationship, because it tends to involve the victim and rescuer both in a little drama called "The Cycle of Abuse." Once you're in, it's hard to get out. The drama, which may run for a lifetime, starts with a victim and an abuser. Typically the abuse, which may be physical, emotional, or sexual, begins early in childhood, often at the hands of one's own family. It may continue for many years, even into adulthood, profoundly affecting the personality development of the victim. Victims learn to see themselves as victims and to expect further victimization. It becomes part of their self-image. Having negative expectations and suffering from low self-esteem, they may not even try to protect themselves from further abuse. They learn to see themselves as helpless and not worthy of protection, and they automatically project this image of themselves. So, they continue to be abused.

Victims of abuse learn to relate to abusive people, even, in a way, to be comfortable in such relationships. Thus, they tend to seek out abusive people to relate to, even to marry. At least they know how to relate to such persons. Victims also learn to act like victims. Thus, potential abusers can easily spot them in a crowd. Victims learn to act in ways that may actually induce people to abuse them. It's a lock-and-key relationship: abusive behavior complements victimized behavior. Acting like a victim produces a kind of urge to abuse, even in normally non-abusive people. For example, victims of physical abuse learn to fear their own anger, to suppress it, and to express hostility only in passive-aggressive ways. After all, open expression of anger is likely to bring on more abuse. Five-year-old victims of physical abuse can be so obnoxious and passive-aggressive you may feel a strong urge to slap them. Similarly, little girls who are sexually abused learn to relate to men in a sexualized way. I've seen three-year-olds that were so seductive it was creepy. They've learned to flirt more like a sophisticated thirty-year-old than an innocent toddler. Again, this kind of behavior may attract or even elicit sexual abuse. If you relate to men in a seductive, flirtatious manner, some of them will try to take you up on the proposition they believe is being offered. When you refuse, having not really intended to offer sex, some of them will get pretty forceful about it.

Young girls and women who've been sexually abused may be so desperate for positive male attention that they place themselves in risky relationships and situations in which they find themselves abused all over again. I had a patient who had been molested by her step-father, leaving her with no self-esteem and no ability to evaluate male behavior accurately. At fifteen she so craved love and attention that she accepted the invitation of three boys she knew slightly to get drunk with them. She was gang-raped. She then felt so dirty and ashamed and worthless that she became "wildly promiscuous" (her words). She finally came to see me when she discovered her step-father molesting her own children. (Thus is abuse self-perpetuating, the gift that goes on giving.)

What all this means is that victims easily become entrapped in a cycle of repetitive abuse. There's another aspect to the cyclical nature of abuse as well. Most abusers started out as victims. One of the worst injuries done by abuse is to impart a feeling of helplessness. The victim is out of control of the situation and can't stop bad things from happening to him. This tends to produce a kind of "trauma-binding," a powerful emotional connection to the abusive events. These emotions may recur in intense flashbacks later in life, memories which replay as if they were truly happening again. They may trigger panic attacks in situations which resemble those of the abuse or in which victims feel trapped and out of control of events. They may also lead to a compulsive urge to repeat the situation– only this time under the former victim's own control. The easiest way to do this is to abuse someone else. Thus, many, though fortunately not most, victims go on to become abusers themselves. The pattern of abuse is thus passed from one generation to the next; I tracked sexual abuse in one family I worked with for at least five generations. As treatment programs for offenders and victims have discovered, they are both treating the same people.

Victims of abuse long for a champion to rescue them and deliver them to safety. They search out knights in armor (or wet puppy collectors) and cry plaintively for help. Even ancient mythologies, however, recognize the dangers inherent in the rescuer-victim relationship. Rush to the aid of the Sirens and you will surely be dashed against the rocks. Save another person and his spirit is entrusted to you for life. On a long-term basis, the victim-rescuer relationship has a tendency to turn abusive, in several ways. If rescuing forms the basis for the relationship, then in order for the relationship to endure it must continue to center around rescuing. The victim must arrange to continue to be victimized (or otherwise in distress, be it financially, emotionally, legally, or whatever) and therefore in need of more saving. This can become tedious if not downright dangerous. Meanwhile, the poor old rescuer may find his role increasingly tiresome as well. He can't stop rescuing and can't teach the victim to stop needing it. He begins to feel trapped, taken advantage of, and, frankly, abused. He may also feel guilty and mean for feeling this way, which adds to his resentment of the victim. "I'm tired of slaying your dragons and saving your backside," he begins to think. "Rescue yourself."

At this point the rescuer, feeling abused himself, may decide to bail out and leave the victim to her own devices. The victim then feels abandoned, rejected, unloved, and– abused. "You're no knight in armor," she thinks, "just another abuser." Her role as victim reinforced, she trots on in search of another rescuer.

Professional relationships between victims and rescuers can also become abusive in another way. This occurs in relationships between victims and doctors, therapists, ministers, or other professional caretakers when the relationship becomes sexualized or otherwise exploitative. It is common and can happen even to the best-intended caregivers. In psychotherapy, for example, the victim of sexual abuse describes painfully and tearfully the awful experiences she's endured In a very real sense, she may even re-experience these events in the course of the therapy, again leaving her to feel dirty, ashamed, and worthless. She needs comforting and perhaps a friendly hug to reassure her the therapist accepts and values her as a person. Hugging is typically off-limits in therapy, but simple human decency dictates an exception in this case. But hugs can quickly become the routine and may escalate to hand-holding during especially traumatic recitations. The boundaries are gradually shifted and the relationship sexualized. Remember, the victim may already be prone to sexualized relationships, because of her abuse. Finally, the therapist and patient are involved in a frank sexual affair. Therapists (ministers, etc.) may rationalize this to themselves as being in the patient's best interest. "I'll give her the love and affirmation she needs," they believe. They see the sexual relationship as therapeutic, a way to help the patient regain her self-esteem and her trust in men. But psychotherapy works only because firm boundaries make it safe. A sexual relationship between therapist and patient is unethical, if not illegal. It is always abusive, by definition, whether the patient invites it or not. Once again, the rescuer-victim relationship becomes an abuser-victim relationship. "Therapist" becomes "the rapist."

Unfortunately the Cycle of Abuse is all too common, and many people are players in this tragic drama. Notice also that the fore-going discussion implies that nearly anybody can become an actor in this play and can, over time, play any of its roles.

Research suggests that child abuse is exceedingly prevalent in our society, with sexual abuse, for example, occurring in 30 to 40 percent of all female children. The victims are all around us. They are us. The perpetrators, meanwhile, are usually people known to them– friends, dates, family members. Abusers aren't, for the most part, strange, different, psychotic, deranged, or poor and illiterate. They are people we meet daily: businessmen, lawyers, doctors, preachers, therapists. I've personally seen a couple of dozen women who were molested by preachers who were also their fathers.

Here's a set of guidelines for people who find themselves in rescuing relationships:

1. Set and keep to safe, appropriate boundaries, right from the start. Keep the relationship focused on the business at hand. Avoid physical contact and displays of affection or comforting. Don't let it get overly personal. Don't let the victim lure you into doing more than you can or should be doing, take too much of your time, or make inappropriate requests. Remember, it is much harder to establish such boundaries later, after lines have already been crossed.

2. Try to keep the relationship temporary. It is simply too burdensome to spend a lifetime rescuing somebody. Get in, help out, and get out.

3. Rescuing is safer if done on a professional basis. The rules, roles, and expectations are a lot clearer, and the relationship is more nearly mutual.

4. Protect yourself from abuse. Don't bring the

victim home with you, either literally or in terms of the emotional impact on your life. (My mother once allowed an impoverished mental patient to come by the house and pick up some food. He also helped himself to some jewelry.) If the rescuing relationship threatens to drown you emotionally, you're in over your head and should get out of the water.

5. Be realistic about your limitations and your expectations from the relationship. Don't try to save the world and don't expect too much in return for your efforts.

6. Keep a friend or colleague as a consultant to you, someone outside and objective to give you feedback and advice. This person will see the relationship more clearly and spot the dangers more quickly because she or he is not emotionally involved.

7. Don't marry somebody you have rescued until you are on a completely equal basis. It would help if he could rescue you a time or two. Then relate as independent equals.

Incidentally, it is very much possible for an abuse victim to break out of the cycle of abuse. You do it by becoming a different kind of person—namely, a survivor instead of a victim. "Survivors" are people who have been victimized in the past, but have overcome the abuse. They have come to realize that they need not internalize the abuse and make it a part of themselves. They no longer feel dirty or ashamed or inferior or unlovable because they recognize that the abuse is not something about them, but rather something about the abuser. It wasn't their fault, wasn't because of anything they said, or did, or were. It's just something that happened to them, not something about them. Once they stop seeing themselves as victims, survivors no longer desire or wish for a rescuer. They'd just as soon take care of themselves. They no longer act like victims or elicit abuse. This makes them a lot less likely to get into the relationship messes we've been looking at.

The lady I described earlier was a rather mousey little soul, small and timid and easily hidden in a crowd. She debated and worried for weeks about what to do, then finally went down to the police station and filed charges against her step-father, not only for molesting her kids, but for abusing her as well. The case went nowhere, as the kids didn't want to testify against their grandpa, and her own abuse was thirty years old. But the impact on her was spectacular. Instead of shrinking shyly into my office, as usual, she strode in confidently, head up and looking me straight in the eye. I knew at once what she'd decided to do and said, "You did it." "I sure as hell did," she replied, in a most uncharacteristic fashion. I'd swear she had grown six inches taller, and for the first time it occurred to me that she was actually quite an attractive lady. She also was a victim no longer. What happens legally when you stand up for yourself is beyond your control, and justice is by no means assured.

The impact on your self-respect, however, is guaranteed. Therapy can help a lot. If you've been abused, get some help and escape the Cycle.

Chapter Four. Mental and Religious Strategies
The Way of Spirituality:

So far we've been looking at strategies for happiness that focus on pleasure-seeking, power, or service. They are all oriented to the world around us, or to ourselves in the world. Now we look at strategies dealing with the mind or with "higher realities." It is possible to make yourself happy by devoting yourself to God or to related spiritual pursuits. This approach may not be for everybody, however. There are many variations on the path of spirituality, and they can lead to quite different lifestyles. For some people the spiritual life means the ordained ministry and life as a parish priest, rabbi, or youth minister. There is enormous variation in lifestyles, of course, even within the ministerial life. Some ministers are as much administrators or business-persons as they are spiritual leaders. Some ministers are teachers, counselors, musicians, or television personalities. In practice, then, the way of spirituality may be combined with other strategies for happiness, such as the ways of service or fame. What provides a common link, however, is that they are all done in God's name or for the furtherance of a religious or spiritual purpose. Most commonly, the ministerial life involves service to others, but again, done in a spiritual or religious context. As we've already noted, Mother Theresa lived a life of service, but she clearly saw herself serving God, not just mankind. We must remember, of course, that the way of spirituality is not limited to the active ministry, but is also practiced by many lay persons in a great variety of ways. Volunteer work, Bible study, yoga, and meditation may all be considered part of the way of spirituality.

In contrast to the service-oriented approach, other paths on the way of spirituality take one not further into the world, but rather away from it. Theologians, for example, devote themselves to the study of spiritual or religious matters. Theirs can be a relatively solitary pursuit, a life of thinking, reading, and writing. They are academicians, not caretakers, and their concerns are often other-worldly and eternal rather than pragmatic or timely. This approach to the way of spirituality could be considered a sub-variant of the **Way of Knowledge.** This is the path to happiness adopted by scientists, philosophers, and some writers. Happiness is to be derived from the accumulation of knowledge, the discovery of truth, the development of the body of science. The Way of Knowledge, including spiritual knowledge, is an intellectual pursuit, which limits its applicability to literate, intelligent individuals. At the same time, the vast majority of people can happily pursue and benefit greatly from a Bible study course, attend Sunday School or learn to meditate. Thus, this version of the spiritual path does not have to be exclusive of other approaches to happiness or limited to some small elite group. Actually, some theologians have even managed to achieve fame and a reasonable standard of living, for example. Can this way of spirituality make you happy? It surely can, for those who love learning and the intellectual life. Indeed, one can hardly read Teilhard de Chardin, for example, without basking in the glow of a truly happy person.

Other approaches to the spiritual life involve a more total commitment and often a more radical withdrawal from everyday life as well. These involve a life of monastic prayer or meditation in which one interacts mainly with the Infinite rather than one's fellow humans. In this approach one may have no job, per se, and often no family life to contend with. It means an essentially solitary life, a life of silent prayer or quiet contemplation. Worldly goods, even relationships may be eschewed as impediments or distractions from one's primary purpose, which is communion with God (or some alternate version of the Infinite.) The Buddhist and Hindu religions have particularly strong traditions for a life of spirituality. To over-simplify greatly, in these religions salvation is attained by achieving enlightenment, the profound realization of one's inclusion within the Universal Soul or consciousness. One's individual soul– Atman in the Hindu beliefs– is a manifestation of the universal soul– Brahman. There are many and various paths to enlightenment (especially in Hinduism) but in essence they involve a kind of drawing inward, away from the world, and engaging in some form of meditation. A trance-like state of altered consciousness may be achieved, perhaps by repetitive prayer, perhaps by fasting, perhaps by contemplation of religious paradoxes (as in Zen Buddhism.) In the Hindu way of Yoga, rigorous bodily training and supreme concentration become a form of meditation, leading to enlightenment.

Judaeo-Christian traditions also include a life of silent prayer, meditation, or contemplation, and maybe self-discipline such as fasting. The popularity of the ascetic or contemplative lifestyle has waned dramatically since the Middle Ages, but cloistered abbeys and monasteries still exist for this purpose. Meanwhile, meditation is commonly practiced in the West, as in the East and has actually made something of a resurgence in recent decades. It has even been secularized and developed into "Transcendental Meditation" and related forms of psychotherapy. Proponents of these practices claim to achieve both peace and happiness now, in this world, as well as salvation in the next.

Are they right? Does the way of spirituality offer a valid, workable program for leading a happy life? It's a complex question, with no one clear and universal answer. Some people turn to a life of spirituality to escape from mundane reality and avoid the hassles, dangers, temptations, or frustrations of life in the world. Monks don't have to compete for jobs, mates, scholarships, or positions on a ball club. They don't have to worry about bills, job security or pension plans; they're set for life. On the other hand, they also sacrifice much of what people find pleasurable, meaningful, and joyful in life. No sex, no marriage, no kids, no new car. It isn't all bad, but it isn't all good either, and it's certainly not for everyone. A spiritual life can be contented and calm or it can be boring, even stressful in itself. Life isn't that easily avoided, and avoidance behavior always carries a heavy price in and of itself. Again we look to motivation. Spiritual withdrawal as an avoidance tactic is doomed to failure, while a positive attraction to the monastic life is a reasonable alternative to the "rat race" most of us run.

There are studies indicating higher rates of depression, schizophrenia, and other mental illnesses amongst the priests, nuns, and other clergy than in the general public. However, cause and effect aren't clear in this regard. It seems highly likely that some people select a religious vocation precisely because they already are either disturbed or at risk for a breakdown and are seeking a safe haven. Highly schizoid (unemotional, socially detached) individuals may be naturally drawn to the monastery, for example, because they phobically avoid interpersonal relationships. Some of these will become increasingly withdrawn and experience a psychotic break, while others will be protected from one by this quiet, safe environment. The same may be said of depressed or obsessive-compulsive individuals. In other words, the spiritual life may not cause mental illness or unhappiness but may attract people already at high risk. Further, a spiritual life is not without its own kinds of stresses, and members of the clergy may not have the support group they need to cope with them. They are also held to a higher standard than the rest of us, yet they are just as human. Certainly there's enough unhappiness available so that one local denomination runs all its potential ministers past me for a psychological evaluation, before they're accepted into the seminary.

For persons well-suited to it, the spiritual way can bring profound joy, meaningfulness, and contentedness. Such persons know theirs is a life with a higher purpose. They are able to let go of the illusory temptations, pleasures, and distractions of life and address matters of ultimate concern. Indeed it is probably essential for all of us to deal in some way, to some degree, with the spiritual side of ourselves and our lives. Physicians now recognize the importance of their patients' spirituality as a health issue. The holistic approach to medicine is a bio-psycho-socio-spiritual one, emphasizing the interplay of these aspects of ourselves and the need to address all of them in treatment. There's even pretty good evidence that strong religious beliefs and prayer can speed recovery from major illness or surgery. **Healthy, happy people tend to be well-rounded and balanced. They develop all facets of their personalities and confront all areas of life.** Thus, some version of the way of spirituality is available to and important for all of us. Being a spiritual person means addressing matters of ultimate concern, seeing ourselves and our lives in perspective and avoiding narcissistic self-absorption. It is at least a part of an effective plan for leading a happy life.

A last note: We should remember that the Way of Spirituality does not necessarily involve any organized religion in belief, practice, or membership. While many people do exercise their spiritual muscles in church work, formal worship services, or within the context of a traditional dogma, for many others spirituality is a private, highly personalized matter. For that matter, there are highly religious people who are not really very spiritual, just as there are spiritual ones who do not subscribe to any organized faith. It's the soul that counts.

The Way of Art:
Very similar to, and sometimes synonymous with the way of spirituality, is the way of art. I use the term broadly, of course, to indicate a life devoted to music, literature, dance, sculpture, painting, or any other form of Art. The similarity to the way of spirituality is that both paths seek to discover truth and beauty and both involve dedicating oneself to the pursuit of a higher purpose than one's own pleasure or prosperity. The sometime synonymity is that for many art and spirituality are the same pursuit: God **is** truth and beauty, and love of God is expressed artistically. As with the spiritual life, an artistic vocation can take

many and varied forms. It can be a total preoccupation, even a driving obsession, or be a part-time hobby. It can also overlap with other ways to happiness, for example, by making one famous. A few people– very few– even get rich at it, though mostly posthumously.

There are certainly problems and disadvantages associated with a life devoted to art. Indeed it is almost axiomatic that the artist must suffer in order to mature artistically. If art is to express the height and depth of the human condition it must transcend the ordinary, and the artist must experience both agony and ecstasy in his own life. An artist must be able to see, hear, and feel life differently– more sensitively, more passionately, than others do. This can hurt. Fortunately, our high-tech, mass-production, consumer-oriented culture and economy virtually ensure that a dedicated artist will suffer, at least financially. Hence the term "starving artist" attached to displays of third-rate, mass-produced paintings. In modern times it is no longer good enough to be very good at one's art to make a good living; one must be extraordinarily good, as well as exceptionally lucky. A few find wealth and fame, especially in the performing arts. The rest find a "day job" to support themselves and pursue their art after work. (My brother and I are psychologists during the week, but on weekends he plays bluegrass music, while I cultivate bonsais. My sister and her husband show apartments and run computers to finance their dancing and acting.)

Most art forms demand a great deal of time in learning the forms, mastering technique, and practicing to near perfection. While many are highly social and exciting (such as music), other art forms are solitary and often tedious pursuits. Painting, for example, is typically a solo performance, and even the musician must practice for long hours alone. Loneliness can be a problem. The hours and working conditions aren't always ideal, either. Sculptors may inhabit cold, bleak studios, while musicians bang around in smoke-filled honky-tonks half the night.

Finally, there is always the very real possibility that your art will be rejected by your audience, leaving you emotionally crushed and probably broke after years of blood, sweat, and tears. In fact, the better you are, the more original and creative, the more likely your productions will initially meet with disapproval, by critics and general public alike. Ask Beethoven, Martha Graham, or Van Gogh. Ask James Joyce. To be fair, we should note that Galileo had a rough time on the Way of Knowledge, and religious martyrs, by definition, come to an untimely end, too. Artists aren't the only ones who experience rejection or disapproval.

So where does the happiness part come in? It comes from discovering a new way to see the world, a new understanding of life and its meaning. It comes from creating something beautiful. It comes from expressing something in one's own unique voice and sharing one's deepest feelings and perceptions with others. It comes from imagining a vision of perfection, struggling to achieve it and finally realizing it in artistic creation. Sometimes it comes from the roar of an audience or a critic's favorable review and the realization that you've communicated with an informed and appreciative public. Happiness comes from the pure fun of doing something well and sharing it with another. Can a life devoted to Art bring you happiness? Sure it can. Can it bring you unhappiness, even tragedy? Yes, that, too. For the Way of Art to work, you must pursue your art for its own sake, not for financial remuneration, fame, or attention. This, of course, is just what we've seen to be true with other ways of being happy. Meanwhile, it's also a good idea to keep your day job until your artistic success is imminent.

Chapter Five. Psychological Strategies
Psychological Strategies:

For some people, their strategy for finding happiness is not so much an approach to living as a way of being. Their strategy is to develop a certain personality style and live it to the hilt. Often this is a personality trait held to some extent by all persons. Often it is a defense mechanism carried to extreme. We've actually dealt with one of these already, in our look at Narcissism. One could probably identify a large number of these psychological strategies, but we'll limit ourselves to the most common few.

The Way of Passivity:

I've said that people adopt a more-or-less conscious strategy for achieving happiness, but there's a kind of exception to this rule. There are people whose strategy is essentially to do nothing and hope for the best. If they can't be happy, at least they may be able to avoid as much of life's unpleasantness as possible. And maybe someone or something will come along to make them happy, if they wait long enough. These individuals don't seek to achieve because they fear failure. They don't seek to exercise power (at least actively) because they fear responsibility and don't trust their own decision-making. They doubt their artistic potential and see themselves as too weak or dependent to take care of others. If anything, they seek only to be taken care of. Theirs is the Way of Passivity.

Passive people sit back and let life happen to them; they don't act, they react. They are insecure, seeing themselves as impotent, helpless, and inadequate. So they don't try to do things but rather to avoid doing. They rarely take the initiative to even make decisions, preferring to let others do so. They are afraid to take chances and will go to great lengths to avoid scary or threatening situations, even where there is a great potential for a positive outcome. Fearing to do for themselves, they try to depend on others to do things for them. Afraid of displeasing others, they cannot be assertive, but instead express themselves in passive-aggressive ways.

Passive people often see themselves as inadequate, and they superficially appear to be so. Yet, paradoxically, there can be enormous power in passivity. As a life strategy it is surprisingly clever and effective at times, though it usually ends up producing a fair amount of unhappiness as well, both for the individual and for those involved with him. I first became aware of the power of passivity in counseling a married couple some years ago. The wife, an active, energetic, and enthusiastic person, insisted that her husband change in certain ways. A passive, almost lethargic person, the husband was afraid to seek a better job, mistrusted his ability to be a father, and was hesitant to borrow the money for a new home. Eager for motherhood, feeling cramped in their small house, and fearful of the imminent demise of her automobile, the wife struggled in vain to motivate and activate her spouse. His style of arguing was also quite passive: she'd raise an issue and he'd either ignore her, avoid the issue or simply stonewall her. He never raised an issue himself, and his customary answer to her was, "I just don't know." The wife was the primary bread-winner and it was she who paid the bills, maintained the house, and initiated sex. As they went round and round in therapy, he seemed relatively content, despite her badgering and fussing, while she became increasingly frustrated and angry. Nothing moved him. I began to realize that for her to "win" or get what she wanted she had to get him to change. For him to win, all he had to do was do nothing. Now pretty clearly, it's easy to do nothing and impossible to change somebody else. He was holding the winning hand. Indeed, the way of passivity could almost be considered a reverse corollary of the way of power, played from the one-down instead of the one-up position.

I am by no means the first to discover this, by the way. Passive resistance, for example, is an incredibly powerful political tool, discovered by Jesus, Gandhi, Martin Luther King, Jr., the Union movement and the leaders of student sit-ins, to name a few. It is generally not an effective short-term strategy, of course, and it exacts an enormous toll on its users, but in the long run it is often highly efficacious. All of the leaders named above were assassinated, for example. Yet the followers of Jesus took control of the Roman Empire within a few hundred years; Gandhi won independence for India; and King's work led to civil rights legislation which radically changed American life and improved the lot of his people. A few hippies got their heads banged, but they eventually got us out of the war in Vietnam. Passive-resistance on the interpersonal level can be as powerful as on the political level, but again it requires patience and the ability to endure the efforts of others to change you, as well as their anger. It can get you what you want, but the price may be pretty high, especially as your frustrated friends and relatives abandon you. Overall, it's not generally the high road to happiness.

Passive-Resistance:

The Way of Passivity is exercised in several different ways: **Passive-Resistance** is the art of not changing or moving so that somebody else must do so. The lunch-counter sit-ins of the civil rights movement are examples, as are the student strikes of the anti-war protestors. Hunger strikes are another form of passive-resistance. These are all ways of saying, "I won't move until you change." Note that there may be a hint of hostility here, the at-least implied notion that you are wrong and I am right and therefore you should feel guilty or ashamed. There's clearly an element of coercion, too; you must change yourself to suit my wishes.

Passive-Aggressiveness:

Hostility is even more prominent in **Passive-Aggressiveness**, the art of expressing anger in subtle, indirect, passive ways. This is what people do when they want to express anger or hurt someone but they aren't comfortable with doing so openly. Any kind of aggressiveness means doing something to hurt somebody. I'm mad at you so I smack you in the face with a pie. But if I'm afraid of you or I believe it unseemly to express hostility so openly, I may find a different way to hurt you and to communicate my feelings. I prepare your favorite pie but purposely screw it up, substituting vinegar for lemon or salt for sugar. I serve it to you lovingly then watch while you gag on it. That's passive-aggressiveness.

Passive-aggressiveness is a way of hurting somebody without having to take responsibility for it. It works fine in the short run, because the other person is hurt but can't retaliate. It was just an accident and you're so apologetic. But passive-aggressiveness always backfires in the long run. I once had a secretary who was a perfect typist, fast and accurate. Yet she'd occasionally hand me a letter full of typos as she left for the day. She'd smile and apologize, but she could not stay late, so I'd have to retype it myself. She "got" me and we both knew it, but I never even found out why she was mad at me. Worse yet, she'd purposely triple-book me, leaving me to apologize myself to two angry patients. Eventually I had to let her go, a shame because she was good and I liked her. Passive-aggressiveness is sneaky and cowardly, and people don't like it, They'll usually find a way to counter-attack. Passive-aggressiveness is often thought of as a feminine trait, but it is not inherently so. It is a tactic used by persons who come from a position of relative weakness, whether physically, societally, or economically. Traditionally, this would include women, but it could also include African-Americans, various immigrant groups, etc. All slaves throughout history, whether the Greeks enslaved by the Romans or the Africans enslaved by the American colonists, are considered to be lazy, shiftless, passive, and a bit dull. That is, they are passive-aggressive, the only way a slave can possibly express anger without being beaten. I noted above the passive-aggressive behavior of abused children. There's sometimes a cultural element here, too. For example, in the South it is considered inappropriate, even low-class, for women to be openly angry or hostile. So they resort to passive-aggressiveness. For a veritable caricature of passive-aggressiveness, study Scarlet O'Hara in "Gone with the Wind."

Dependency:
    Dependency is another way of living passively, and there are people who purposely render themselves incompetent, helpless, or disabled so that somebody else must cake care of them. An extreme example of this is noted later in this book,

looking at dependency in marriage, by way of a lady so dependent she couldn't set her own watch. The problem is that dependency always includes an element of control, and control generally leads to resentment and anger. The passive-dependent person forces you to take care of him, or to feel guilty for not doing so. Naturally, you resent him either way. For some people dependency is a conscious and calculated strategy. Malingerers, for example, fake illness to receive unnecessary medical care and disability payments. People with "factitious disorders," such as Munchausen's Syndrome, go one step further. They actually make themselves sick by ingesting poisons, infecting themselves with bacteria, even injecting their own feces under their skin. Others accomplish the same goal but actually do so unconsciously, by turning emotional distress into debilitating physical illnesses. This is called a "conversion reaction" (formerly called "conversion hysteria"). It has become rare in our psychologically sophisticated times, but I've actually seen two cases of hysterical blindness in which patients became completely disabled and dependent through a blindness that had no physiological cause. These people had to be led everywhere by the hand and were waited on hand and foot by their families, because they could not see. Yet their eyes were in perfect working order; their problem was strictly psychological. At some unconscious level these people did not want to see.

Avoidance:

Another variation on a life of passivity is the pattern of **Avoidance**. There are a lot of scary things in the world out there, things that can hurt or even kill you. We read every day in the newspaper of people dying on the highway, either in hideous crashes or at the hands of road-enraged fellow motorists. Kids are shooting up the schools and tornadoes blowing them down. It's realistic to be afraid. Yet, most of us pull in our guts, stick out our chins, and get on about the business of living anyway. We drop the kids at school and take the freeway to the office with barely a glance at the weather channel on the way out the door.

Avoiders take a different approach, or, more accurately, a retreat. Rather than confront fearful situations head-on and learn to conquer their fears, they go to great extremes to avoid them. This works fine at the time, but as a long-term strategy it is sorely wanting. Avoiding scary situations often means losing out on potentially rewarding ones as well. Going to college is scary; getting married is frightening; and having children is absolutely terrifying. Yet these are three of life's most meaningful and rewarding ventures. Avoiding them means you won't fail, get hurt or be rejected, but you won't win or be loved either. Typically, the riskiest investments also have the highest rates of return, but if you venture nothing you gain the same.

The pattern of avoidance has a tendency to generalize, as does obsessive- compulsiveness.

Eventually it becomes increasingly cumbersome and inconvenient and can be utterly incapacitating. I once saw a fellow who'd had a panic attack as he happened to be driving across a bridge. As a result, he developed a secondary phobia of bridges. It began with that bridge only, but quickly spread to all large bridges and then to smaller and smaller ones. By the time I saw him he couldn't drive into his mother's driveway because it ran over the culvert for a drainage ditch. He was driving fifty miles out of the way to avoid a bridge a few blocks from home and he couldn't drive on the interstates or freeways at all. (Think about it... They're just a series of ramps and overpasses, i.e. bridges). Avoiding bridges had him constantly anxious and practically unable to go anywhere.

Avoidance has a self-perpetuating tendency as well. Because avoiding a scary situation reduces anxiety, it is self-rewarding and therefore prone to continue. Further, there is never an opportunity to confront and thus to overcome the fear, since the situation is successfully avoided. You can unlearn your fear of the water either by inching very slowly into the baby end of the pool, staying calm and gradually going deeper, or by diving into the deep end. The former technique is slow but involves minimal anxiety. The latter is fast but briefly terrifying. Either will work, and both are used clinically. The gradual approach is called "systematic desensitization" and the latter is "implosion." Both ways will work, but please note that both involve getting wet. The avoider never gets wet and therefore never conquers her fear. I've seen avoiders who were finally forced by circumstances to confront the situation they'd feared and shunned for years. They were amazed to find that it wasn't all that bad. In fact, it wasn't nearly as bad as the fear itself or the inconvenience of the avoidance maneuvers. An old friend of my wife's decided to overcome her life-long fear of the water and take swimming lessons. She loved it and is still an avid swimmer.

An even more pathological form of avoidance is the effort to selectively avoid certain "bad" feelings. For example, children who have been abused physically often learn to fear their own anger. After all, they've experienced anger mainly in connection with being beaten by angry parents. Further, if they allowed themselves to feel angry, they might inadvertently express their anger, and this would lead to even worse abuse. So they try to block their anger and not even to feel it themselves. This is likely to raise your blood pressure in addition to alienating you from your own emotional life. It also denies you an emotion that is a useful self-motivator and an essential psychological defense mechanism.

Similarly, people who have been sexually abused come to fear their own sexual desires or arousal and try to block these feelings, along with associated feelings of shame, guilt, and disgust. Thus, they are deprived of sexual pleasure and an important part of a marital relationship. They may even lose the marriage altogether, if they are even capable of getting into one in the first place.

I've even treated patients who tried to block *all* good feelings, believing themselves unworthy of them or realizing that the capacity to feel joy entails also the capacity to feel sorrow. These people end up in a kind of semi-death wherein they feel essentially nothing at all. This is experienced as a numbness, a lack of real being, or a kind of chronic low-grade depression. To some folks, however, this is preferable to allowing one's self to *feel*, and therefore to experience pain. We'd all like to block out the bad feelings and feel only the good ones. Unfortunately, it is a package deal: feeling love, joy, triumph, and pleasure means you also get hate, sorrow, failure, and pain. Some people, unfortunately, are too scared to pay the price.

People who fear and seek to avoid their own feelings are at risk for developing Panic Disorder, which might be thought of as a fear of fear itself. In the attempt to block their feelings, such individuals are often unaware of them until they are pretty intense and, thus, frightening. When human beings become alarmed, their bodies react automatically, preparing them to handle a presumably life-threatening emergency. Say you're strolling through the jungle and stumble nose-to-nose onto a ferocious tiger. You've got several options to avoid being eaten:
1. You can fall down in a faint, convincing the tiger you are dead. Maybe he won't eat you, since tigers

prefer their meat live and on-the-hoof. This is what possums do. In fact, I've been told possums even simulate death by smelling like carrion. This primitive fainting instinct is still hard-wired in human neural programming. At one time it was very fashionable to swoon in a crisis, though now it has become passe.

2. You can beat up the tiger, thereby preventing him from turning you into the luncheon special.

3. You can run away from the tiger. Successfully carried out, any of these tactics will keep you from being consumed by the tiger, but only the fight or flight tactics are actually available to most people.

Either fighting or fleeing necessitates increased oxygen flow to the muscles for the burning of more energy. Thus, our lungs automatically begin to breathe more rapidly and our hearts to pump faster, bringing more oxygenated blood to the muscles. Blood flow is diverted away from the head and the gut to the limbs. After all, it doesn't take a lot of brain power to run or to slug somebody. And you don't need to be digesting your lunch while running from a predator; indeed, it's even better if you can eliminate the dead weight, increasing your speed and your chances of not becoming *his* lunch. (It's better yet if you can throw-up *on* the tiger. He may be so disgusted he leaves you alone. Monkeys in this situation will defecate and *throw* it at the tiger.) All of this is done automatically by the autonomic nervous system (ANS). Subjectively these changes are experienced as being out of breath, having heart palpitations, a warm flushing all over, mild nausea, and light-headedness. Some people also find their thought processes impaired and some experience a kind of tunnel vision. And all these sensations are also accompanied by an intense, overwhelming feeling of fear or panic.

Now all these feelings are the result of perfectly normal physiological adaptations, and no one would think twice about them when truly facing a real tiger. What is so disconcerting and confusing about panic disorder, however, is that all this occurs in the absence of any tigers. The activation of the fight or flight response is itself frightening when no tiger is present. Many people will immediately assume they are having a heart attack, though they are not.

So what's going on with this panic disorder, to make people react as if they were confronting a dangerous animal when none is there? Well, the answer is that there *is* a tiger to be dealt with, only it's a *psychological* rather than a physical beast. Something is perceived to be a life-threatening emergency, even though the threat exists only in one's mind. It may be something you see, a memory coming back to you, an idea or thought or even a dream (Yes, it can even happen in your sleep.), but some mental event triggers the panic attack. This happens because the autonomic nervous system has no direct connection to the outside world, but receives its marching orders from the central nervous system. Thus, it can't distinguish between real and psychological tigers. If your brain says "tiger alert" your body reacts. Since the triggering thought is often quite fleeting, the panic sufferer is often consciously unaware of it. The first thing he notices is that his body is going berserk. This often sets up an escalating feedback loop, as he may misinterpret the ANS arousal as a heart attack, seizure, or other medical emergency. He thinks, "I'm dying," which truly is a scary thought. This thought triggers even more ANS arousal, which convinces him the heart attack is real, and so on.

All sorts of thoughts or feelings can trigger panic attacks, as we've already noted. Some people panic when they begin to feel angry. I saw a lady who panicked whenever she felt sexy. It turned out she was attracted to someone and was afraid she'd have an affair and destroy her marriage. Multiple personality patients panic when long-repressed memories of childhood abuse begin to resurface. However, in my experience, the two most common triggers of panic attacks are feeling trapped and feeling abandoned. (I am indebted to Dr. Les Alhadeff for helping me to recognize this.) That's why people experience panic attacks in crowded malls or come to fear leaving home. (This is called agoraphobia and is a secondary complication of panic disorder, in reaction to having panic attacks in public places.) I saw a corporate vice president who panicked in board of directors meetings, feeling trapped and suffocated by them. Granted, they were undoubtedly highly political, tedious, or even mind-numbing, but boredom is rarely considered a life-threatening emergency.

Incidentally, panic disorder is generally quite treatable with medications and psychotherapy. In the short run tranquilizers and sometimes antidepressants can be very effective in controlling the attacks. They provide some immediate relief and demonstrate that there is hope for sufferers of this disorder. Unfortunately some of these medications are expensive and some are habit-forming, so they may not provide a long term solution. However, most panic patients can learn to head off or control their attacks. The first step is to get your body calmed down enough for you to think clearly again. In a panic attack you are hyperventilating, that is breathing rapidly but shallowly. You feel as if you need to take in more air, but in truth your lungs are full and you need to empty them and then resume normal breathing. You can signal your body to do this either by breathing in and out of a paper bag (i.e. rebreathing the same air) or by holding your breath for a while. Either way you increase the carbon dioxide level in your lungs, the signal to exhaust them and breathe in again. I prefer holding your breath, as it's faster, doesn't require any equipment, and doesn't look as goofy. Hold it for thirty seconds, if you can, then let the air come rushing out all at once. Muscle tension and release also tend to relax the body and can be done simultaneously with the breath-holding. A quick, easy exercise of this type is what I call "The

Incredible Hulk," after the old television series: Make a tight fist with both hands and tense all the muscles in your arms and chest and shoulders, posing like a body-builder (or The Hulk). Let your muscles relax quickly, as you breathe out. Then distract yourself from the scary triggering thought by counting to fifty and reminding yourself that this is just normal ANS arousal and you're not going to die.

Then comes the really hard part, rethinking the scary thought or psychological "tiger" so it no longer appears to you a life-threatening emergency. But now you can do it, because you're calmer and can think clearly again. Psychotherapy can help tremendously in the effort to de-fang and de-claw the tiger. In therapy you come to see that you're not truly trapped– you've got options and can usually escape or deal with an unpleasant but not life-threatening problem. If the Board meeting gets too gruesome, excuse yourself and go to the bathroom, for example. You're probably not totally rejected and abandoned either, but just feeling that way because one friend let you down on this one occasion (which perhaps recapitulates in your unconscious mind the time your Mom lost you in the store when you were three). In therapy you learn to deal with your feelings, to moderate and modulate or simply endure them until they go away.

The Way of "Love":
This one requires a little extra explanation. We're not talking here of people who love God, people who love music or science or money, not even of people who love their spouses (who we'll look at more closely in the second part of this book). What I want to examine here is those folks who believe that a relationship is both necessary and sufficient to make them happy. These are people who are in love with being in love. Sometimes they select a particular target, believing only that one person can make them happy. Other times their desire is more generic and anyone will do. But for these folks a one-on-one loving relationship is the sine qua non of happiness. As Gracie Slick sang with the Jefferson Airplane:

> "Do you want somebody to love?
> Don't you need somebody to love?
> Wouldn't you love somebody to love?
> You better find somebody to love."

Or, in the words of the song which inspired this book's title: "Love is the answer; someone to love is the answer."

Unfortunately, love is not always the answer, but there's no way to convince devotees of this Way, despite their own bitter experiences with relationships. Ironically, the most fervent believers tend to be people with a long history of disastrous relationships. **Rather than recognizing that a relationship is not the key to happiness, these people believe they simply haven't found the**

right one. So they keep on frantically looking for the perfect lover. People with Borderline Personality Disorder are probably the most extreme example of the breed, so we'll use them as an illustrative case study.

Borderline Personality Disorder:
By definition, these poor souls experience "a pattern of unstable and intense interpersonal relationships," as well as "a markedness and persistently unstable self-image or sense of self." (From the American Psychiatric Association's DSM-IV 1994) That is, they are not comfortable alone or with others. "Borderlines" are mostly women, constituting, in a sense, the female equivalent of the typically male narcissistic and antisocial personality types (though it's an equal opportunity thing and both sexes may be diagnosed with any of these personality disorders.) They have no clear idea of who they are and therefore they try to define themselves relative to others. They see themselves as somebody's daughter, somebody's girlfriend, somebody's wife, or somebody's mother, but never as *somebody* in their own right. When they are alone they experience a profound sense of emptiness, because now they are *nobody*. They *have* to have a relationship to tell them who they are, fill up the emptiness and make them feel alive and well. So they attach themselves desperately to whomever will have them and hang on for all they're worth. But they are suspicious, and given

enough stress, can become frankly paranoid, doubting their own lovability and thus the sincerity of the other's love for them. They strive frantically to avoid real or imagined abandonment and may experience panic attacks or make suicidal gestures when they feel rejected. They become possessive and controlling and become furious if their mate refuses to cater to their every whim or, worse yet, tries to have an independent existence.

Just as they have no clear sense of self, people with borderline personality disorders have little insight into the motivation or character of their partners. Thus, they tend to select inappropriate and often abusive mates who look good, but aren't. Then they tend to alternate between extremes of idealization and devaluation of the other. One minute they're in love and you're the most wonderfullest person in the whole wide world. The next they're in hate and you've become a scum-sucking swine, though you've done absolutely nothing different. This is pretty disconcerting, even distressing, to the mate, who has no way to predict the moods or behavior of the borderline. Borderlines also tend to try to control their wild mood swings through impulsive, addictive, and self-destructive behaviors such as binge eating, sexual promiscuity and self-mutilation. If you're in a relationship with someone with a borderline personality, fasten your seat belt and keep your insurance paid up. They're sexy and exciting, but they can make your life a lot more interesting than you can handle. If they become bored, for example, they will literally pick a fight with you just for the excitement.

It's not at all clear what causes some people to develop borderline personalities. (The name, incidentally, refers to a now out-dated theory and isn't really very meaningful anymore.) There may be hereditary factors at work, in addition to early life experiences. A simplistic but comprehensible way of looking at it is to say that the borderline person is emotionally fixated at an age when infants are first developing a sense of Self versus Other. If a baby cries and Mother feeds him, this is perceived as a "Good Mother" experience. If the mother fails to nurture the infant, or responds inappropriately (such as changing his diaper when he's hungry), this is a "Bad Mother" experience. It appears that early on the infant actually seems to separate or "split" these two sets of experiences in his mind, as if they involved two entirely different mothers. Only later does he realize that the good and bad mothers are one and the same person, forming a mental image of a single, coherent Other person. Likewise, the baby internalizes these mothering experiences as either "Good Me" or "Bad Me" perceptions, depending on their positive or negative outcomes. In effect, the infant seems to assume that if Mother feeds me, then I must be a good boy or girl, and if she doesn't it indicates I'm a bad person.

Over time there should be a preponderance of Good Mother experiences over Bad Mother episodes, enabling the developing infant to merge the two into one coherent image of a "Good Enough Mother." Mother is seen as a real person, who isn't perfect and sometimes misses the mark, but is good enough to trust and love. This image is generalized to other persons as well, and the infant adopts a basically open and trusting way of relating to others. The good enough mother forms the groundwork for perceiving others as also good enough to love and trust, giving way eventually to good enough friends, lovers, spouses, and so on. Likewise, the internalized self-image also merges Good Me's and Bad Me's into a coherent sense of ones's own self as "good enough." This forms the basis for later self-love or self-esteem, just as the relationship with the mother (or other caretaker) forms the foundation for later loving relationships. Note that in both instances, the image of self or of other is based in reality and provides a realistic description of that individual, not a perfect image no one can live up to. That's why the classic text on self-esteem is entitled "I'm OK, You're OK," and not something like "You're Fantastic and I'm Perfect."

In borderline personalities, unfortunately, the merger never fully occurs. They continue to "split" others into all-good (idealization) or all-bad (devaluation) with nothing in-between. And they split their self-image in the same fashion, alternately seeing themselves as all good or all bad. Their thinking is notoriously black-or-white, with no shades of gray. They have no genuine self-love and therefore are greatly impaired in their ability to love others. They don't like themselves and assume others won't like them either. Predicting rejection, they naturally tend to keep their guard up– and their defenses push others away. They set up a self-fulfilling prophecy, in effect actually causing the rejection and abandonment they so fear. They also are mistrustful of anyone who does seem to love them, suspecting either an ulterior motive or deciding that "anybody who loves a sorry person such as myself can't be much of a person himself," another form of devaluation.

In the most extreme cases, where the "Bad Mother" is truly **bad** the child may even develop a frank multiple personality disorder, splitting off parts of her Self into distinct and separate others or "alters." Actually, I don't mean to pick on mothers here. MPD develops mostly from childhood abuse, and the abuser can be anyone– mother, father, grampa, brother, the kid next door, even some evil cult group. If some of this sounds a bit far-fetched, consider this: a multiple personality patient in her thirties confided in me that she had just begun to realize that the Bad Brother who abused her and the Good Brother who played with her were actually the same human being. Just as she had split herself into a dozen personalities, she had continued to maintain the split perception of her brother she'd learned in childhood. Incidentally, like most MPDs she had "alter" personalities she called "Good Mother" and "Bad Mother," another example of borderline-like splitting. MPD is a highly controversial but intriguing diagnostic category. It's not known how many true cases exist, how many may actually develop in the course of a misguided therapy, or whether some MPDs are simply role-playing. It is pretty clear, however, that most MPDs have some borderline personality traits and experience great difficulties in relationships.

Borderline personalities are the most extreme examples of Love Addicts, but they nicely illustrate, in dramatic form, the kinds of problems anybody can have in relationships and the pitfalls of this Way to happiness. Believing that they **must** have a relationship to make them happy, Love Addicts carom frantically from one all-consuming relationship to another. Since they are desperate, they can't afford to be too selective, so they tend to end up with highly inappropriate matches, then cling to them long past the obvious time to give up and get out. Even when they do get out of the relationship, these individuals can't let go, and they frequently remarry the same abusive husband they just divorced, somehow convincing themselves that he's changed or this time it will work out. I've seen them marry the same jerk three or four times.

Individuals who adopt this way to find happiness expect others to meet all their emotional needs, even to build their self-esteem. They are amazed and infuriated when the other either fails at this impossible task or refuses even to try. The partner is then devaluated if not outright demonized and a new ideal lover is sought after. Thus, their dependency takes on a hostile quality which sabotages the relationship and drives the other away.

The truth is that relationships do not make you happy. Granted, we are social beings and exist in relation to each other. And we have needs that only others can meet for us. But, as we've seen throughout this book, you make your own happiness in life; nobody can do it for you. Most relationships provide a very mixed bag of pain and pleasure, sorrow and joy, rejection and acceptance. In good ones the positive far outweighs the negative, but even the best of relationships have difficult, even painful times. They're not easy to maintain either. They require a great deal of work and attention. They require you to compromise, to change yourself, to enter into another's world and mind. As I tell my patients, if you get close to someone, sooner or later you're going to get hurt. It's the price of admission to intimacy. Some people end up concluding that the price is too high and relationships are too dangerous. They opt to play it safe by never getting close to anyone and living in isolation. That option has its price too, of course; it's called loneliness.

If you do enter into an intimate relationship you realize eventually that your partner is not going to make you happy. If you're going to be happy in a relationship, *you must make yourself happy with your partner.* If you've chosen well and found a good mate, he or she will *help* you to be happy, give you a lot of reasons to be happy, work on being happy with you, and help you meet your needs. But you've still got a job to do. You've got to learn to accept and be happy with your mate *as is*, and quit trying to fix or change him. You've got to learn to respect and even value the way your spouse is different. And you've got to help her meet her own needs in the relationship, needs which may be quite different from your own. Your partner will undoubtedly possess some trait, characteristic, or habit which you may find irritating or obnoxious. If you're going to be happy with him, I recommend you learn to see that trait or behavior as a "lovable eccentricity" rather than an annoying habit.

I see a lot of people who look to a relationship to make them happy, to complete them as a person, to build their self-esteem, to take care of them emotionally, financially, socially and physically, to protect them from a hostile world, to fill up the emptiness they sometimes feel inside, and to eliminate their depression, anxiety, or despair. Not only is this impossible, but seeking a loving relationship from this perspective almost ensures they will make a poor choice of a mate. They end up, in the words of the country song, "Looking for love in all the wrong places." Look for someone strong enough to make you feel safe and secure and you may find yourself married to a controlling or abusive husband. Look for someone sexy and flirtatious enough to build up your self-esteem and make you feel like a real stud and you may end up married to an unfaithful wife who is more interested in making some other guy feel good. Or you may just meet up with another desperately unhappy person who wants *you* to solve all of *their* problems and make them happy.

I tell my unhappy patients to quit looking for somebody to make them happy and take responsibility for that job themselves. If you're single, with no relationship in sight, then figure out how to be happy as a single person. Find ways to entertain yourself so you don't have to depend on others to do so. Learn to be alone without being lonely. Find or create meaning in your life. Join a church, volunteer at a hospice, take a class in astronomy, do some professional writing. Cultivate a bonsai. Don't go out with someone you can't stand just to be going out. Staying home on Saturday night doesn't mean there's something wrong with you, just that you happen not to have a date. On the contrary, it means there's something *right* with you: you've got enough self-respect not to go out with any old jerk. When you're alone, you're in good company. On the other hand, don't refrain from an outing just because the group is mostly couples. Good friends usually won't mind including a singleton. (By the way, if you do take a class, make it something you're genuinely interested in for its own sake. If you join a scuba class just to meet guys and they all turn out to be married, you'll have wasted time and money and you'll be bitterly disappointed.)

What I find truly fascinating is that if you quit searching frantically for someone to make you happy and set about doing it for yourself, a marvelous transformation is like to occur. Learning to make yourself happy is not only useful in and of itself, it actually re-programs your unconscious mind, the part of you that tells you who to fall in love with. Suddenly you're no longer so attracted to the dysfunctional, inappropriate or abusive people you used to cling to so desperately and disastrously. You see them for what they are and not as the answer to any question you might care to ask. Instead, you find yourself drawn to other *happy people*, and often these will be people you formerly ignored, over-looked or even rejected outright as dull, self-centered, stuck-up, or unavailable. You start falling in love with good, happy people you might actually have a chance of building a happy life with.

Beyond this, being a happy person yourself, you'll find that other happy people are drawn to you like bargain-hunters to a garage sale. **Often, when people quit looking desperately for a relationship, a relationship finds them. Happy people are like magnets; they're attracted to each other.** And when they get together they share not their loneliness or depression or self-doubt or demanding needs; they share their happiness. How to make yourself happy in a long-term intimate relationship is the subject of the second half of this book.

-125-

Chapter Six. The Way of Responsibility
The Way of Responsibility:

In our survey of some of the major strategies for achieving happiness we've hit all around but not quite really addressed what is probably the way adopted by most people: The Way of Responsibility. Or perhaps we simply haven't looked at this approach at a general enough level. Actually, all the successful ways we've examined do involve leading a responsible life, whether in terms of helping others, serving God, or creating artistic beauty. The unsuccessful ways involve being irresponsible and letting ourselves become passive, addicted, obsessed, or self-absorbed. **The take-home message here is that happy people are responsible people, a message most people learn eventually.**

Most people don't lead "lives of quiet desperation," but rather lives of purposeful dedication, participation, and perspiration. They have times of depression, anxiety or apathy, but for the most part they get up, perform their morning rituals and go off to work. They do their jobs, collect their pay and come home to their families and their household chores. They schlep the kids to soccer games, reheat Tuesday's meatloaf, supervise homework, and catch the end of the Braves' game before bed. They call Mom to see how she's doing and send Dad a card and a superfluous tie on Father's Day. They go to the beach when they get a chance, meet at Grandma's for Christmas, and try to exercise enough to keep their belt at the same notch. For the most part they are happy, especially on the weekends.

Responsible people go to work every day unless they are truly ill. They give a good day's work and try to take pride in what they do. They care about and are involved with their families and friends. They are involved in and contribute to their communities. They read the paper and cast an informed vote. They give to charity and volunteer their time in community affairs. They pay their bills, enjoy their hobbies, and limit themselves to a few beers (and only when they're not driving). Moreover, they're happy doing all these things.

Why? Partly because they know that responsible behavior pays off in the long run. Putting responsible limits on ourselves actually gives us more freedom, for example. What freedom would we have to drive safely on our roadways if most people didn't obey stop lights and stay somewhere near the speed limits? Similarly, stealing cars is fine while it lasts, but once you're caught (and they're hard to hide) you lose the car as well as your freedom. Buying cars takes effort and patience and costs you in the short run, but in the long run you get a better deal– and you get to keep the car. This is what many of my adolescent patients are struggling to comprehend. They tend to believe that freedom comes from simply being an adult and that the quickest way to get it is to take it. They don't see that freedom is inextricably involved with responsibility. It must be earned. True, responsible behavior typically costs you up front, but it pays off later. Responsible people have learned to defer gratification and end up happy in the long run.

Responsible people feel good about themselves because they know they are doing the right thing. Being a moral, decent, ethical, responsible person costs you sometimes, but you can sleep easy at night, and when you look in the mirror an honest face looks back. In addition, responsible people typically enjoy the respect of their friends, family, and community.

Finally, responsible people tend to figure out how to enjoy being responsible, not just for the long-term benefits, but *now*. They learn to take pride in their work and their accomplishments and enjoy making a contribution to society. They learn to appreciate even that tired feeling that comes from strenuous effort. If you've got to work anyway, why not learn to derive some satisfaction from it? The lawn has to be mowed in any case, so enjoy the good physical workout, revel in being in the great outdoors, do the best job you can, and take pride in a well-trimmed yard.

The Way of Play:

For most of us life is basically about living up to various responsibilities. As I keep telling my kids, it's not mostly about playing; it's about working. I suppose we could list a **Way of Play** as another strategy for finding happiness in life. This would presumably indicate a life devoted solely to playing and having fun. I haven't chosen to deal with this approach at any length mainly because it simply is not available to most of us in any case. This lifestyle would be the opposite of the ways of service or responsibility, a life of sport, leisure, hobbies, or other forms of play. The first problem with it, of course, is who's going to pay for it. For most of us there's no one to pay the bills if we don't do it ourselves, effectively eliminating this approach as a viable option, at least until we reach the age of retirement. There are other people, heirs to huge family fortunes, for example, who do have the option of playing all their lives. How well do they fare? From what I can see of it, these folks don't generally seem to be all that happy. The harder they play, the more meaningless their lives seem to become. They have a difficult time developing any sense of self-esteem, because they do nothing productive, contribute nothing to society and can't possibly accomplish anything remotely equaling the efforts of whoever's money they're living off of. Further, their play often deteriorates into addictive pleasure-seeking, whose pitfalls we've already examined in detail. Or they become famous for being famous and their opulent lifestyle is catalogued and displayed in the tabloid press. I admit I don't often see such publications, and perhaps I'm simply envious, but what I see of this approach to life does not look all that attractive. I do know some people who are wealthy enough to play all the time if they chose to, but the happy ones don't. Instead, they find productive jobs, devote themselves to community service, or find meaning in the pursuit of art, religion, or the other healthy ways we've already examined.

Actually, there's another group of people who manage to follow the way of play, and many do so successfully and happily. These are the professional athletes, musicians, and other performers who get paid to do what they would otherwise be glad to do for fun. As we've already noted, this approach to life is not available to everyone; it requires both exceptional talent and extraordinary luck. And judging from the tabloid press, again, happiness is by no means guaranteed even to these gifted ones. I suspect the ones who do achieve happiness do it by approaching their play as an avocation, a job, a responsibility, even a duty. They live for their art or for their families, not just for the sake of having fun. Pleasure-seeking, as we have already seen, is not the high road to happiness.

The Way of Duty:
For some people, the Way of Responsibility takes a stricter, even harsher form, and becomes the **Way of Duty.** The idea here is not just to live responsibly but to do one's duty as assigned, without fail, without an argument or complaint. Where the duty comes from varies a lot, but it is, by definition, from some higher authority. This may be one's parents, the officers who outrank you, the

State, or society at large. For many people it is the Highest Authority; their duty is imposed on them by God Himself.

Whole societies are based on the Way of Duty as their central cultural norm. It's a pretty efficient way to do business. Everyone knows exactly what is required of them and who's the boss. Everyone knows what penalties must be paid for failure to do one's duty. Life is simple and clear and there's not a lot of conflict or debate. Of course, there may also be limited opportunities for exercising ingenuity, imagination or creativity. A good example of a society built around the way of duty is Japan, especially in times past. Traditional Japanese society was arranged in a rigid hierarchy, from the "Son of Heaven" himself (the Emperor, believed to be divine, and holder of a hereditary position), down through the Samurai or warrior class, down to the lowest "eta" (almost like an untouchable, the lowest class of butchers, tanners, grave diggers, etc.) Each person was owned by the lord to whom he was a vassal, and failure to obey him or do one's duty was the ultimate crime. The punishment was death and disgrace and might be extended to one's entire family as well. Doing one's duty, on the other hand, brought honor and respect, as well as tangible rewards, such as money, land, fine clothing, even entry to the Samurai class or a title. The moral code was essentially the Code of Bushido, which is to say, duty.

Was traditional Japan or "Nippon" a happy

place? Did the Way of Duty work? We can only judge from historical accounts, but it appears the results were somewhat mixed. Medieval Japan developed an extremely sophisticated society and produced great art and craftwork, including the world's finest clothing, swords, gardens, and ceramics. However, it also shut itself off from the rest of the world for centuries and had to import much of its culture from China, a much more open society. Japan was a rigid, closed and generally warlike society with frequent rebellions and civil wars. Its people led harsh lives, for the most part, and death could come at any time, instantaneously, either in battle or at the command– even whim– of one's lord, or at one's own hand. Nowhere has suicide (seppuku) been developed as such an art form as in Japan. On the other hand, there was usually sake (rice wine) aplenty for the more well-to-do, and Japanese sexual practices would make a hippie blush. It would be hard to find a society where appreciation of the arts is so widely spread and thoroughly included in every aspect of daily life as in Japan, at all levels of society. I suspect most people probably were fairly happy in old Japan because Japanese society taught them to enjoy working, to take pride in doing their duty, and to appreciate the beauty of nature, the pleasure of a ceremonial tea, and so on. Most Japanese eventually became Buddhist and learned to accept their karma and live in accord with the ways of nature.

The Way of Duty has its advantages. It tends toward simplicity, clarity, and stability. It also tends to produce rigidity, conformity, anxiety, even stagnation in a society bound by duty. In its more extreme forms, I don't think it works too well for most people. It is too confining and puts one too much at the mercy of others. In contrast to Orientals, who are raised to do their duty, honor their family, and put the needs of society ahead of personal needs, the typical Westerner is a rugged individualist who does someone else's bidding only grudgingly. Doing one's duty feels too controlling to most of us. Further, one is always a bit anxious about whether one is truly doing as she's supposed to, or whether someone is displeased with her. But if you like clear, simple guidelines, don't like to make decisions, and enjoy hard work, the Way of Duty might be just your cup of cha (tea.)

Summary and Conclusions:
There may be an infinite number of ways in which people try to make themselves happy, and I don't pretend to have examined more than a representative sample of them. In a sense you might almost say that each one of us develops his or her own unique plan for happiness, combining elements of the approaches described above and perhaps adding a few new twists as well. Most of us probably change our strategies from time to time also, as we see what doesn't work and develop more sophisticated ideas of what constitutes happiness in

the first place. In our somewhat rambling survey of these strategies for attaining happiness we've seen several that can work well, others that typically don't. What general conclusions can we draw about how to be a happy person? Here's a quick synopsis:

1. **Happiness is self-induced.** You must take responsibility for your life and your happiness. You can't afford to depend on others to make you happy.

2. **Happiness is best sought indirectly.** Do what you need to do, follow your dream, be generous and productive, and let happiness find you as a result. Interestingly, my experience is that most happy people don't think very much about being happy and are not consciously trying to make themselves happy. They're too busy doing their thing to worry about the problem. It's the unhappy ones who are preoccupied with becoming happy.

3. **Real happiness is a long-term proposition**; short-term strategies yield pleasure but not happiness, and they fail in the long run. Yet, the only moment in which you can be happy is the present moment, because only it exists. Thus, you need to keep a balance between enjoying today and saving for tomorrow. It helps to focus on and learn to enjoy the *process* of working towards your goal. If you've got to run a marathon, learn to enjoy the process of running, not just crossing the finish line.

4. **Happiness depends on learning to think rationally, logically, and positively.**

5. **Happy people involve themselves in and become productive members of the Community of Man.**

6. **Happy people develop loving relationships** and relate to others in an open, direct, and honest fashion. Having learned how to make themselves happy, they share their happiness with others.

7. **To achieve true happiness you must devote yourself to something or someone outside yourself** and seek to avoid selfishness or self-absorption.

8. **The act of creation leads to happiness and joy, as does the act of giving.**

9. **In order to be happy you must be true to yourself.** Trying to be someone you're not, do something that just isn't you, won't fool anybody in the long run, and won't bring you happiness.

10. **Responsible, moral behavior leads to happiness.**

As I was writing this section I chanced to read a lovely little book entitled *Tuesdays with Morrie,* that was making the rounds in my Sunday School class. In it Mitch Albom chronicles his last meetings with his old favorite professor, Morrie Schwartz, as his friend and mentor lay dying of amyotrophic lateral sclerosis (Lou Gehrig's Disease). Albom describes Morrie as a happy, loving, and joyful man who refused to lose his zest for life even as his muscles atrophied into total paralysis. I close this section with a quote from Morrie, who managed to cover most of what I've tried to say, in one sentence:

"Devote yourself to loving others, devote yourself to your community around you, and devote yourself to creating something that gives you purpose and meaning." –Morrie Schwartz

I've heard a lot of people say they *can't* be happy, for a wide variety of reasons. They're in chronic pain or they're broke, or their job stinks, and their wife's run off with the guy who repossessed the car. I don't believe it, though I do believe it is much more difficult for some people to be happy than for others, and some situations make it a real challenge, to be sure. But I have an old friend who became president of a huge company and is now an ambassador, not to mention a happy and fun-loving guy, despite being a bilateral amputee. I worked with a young girl born with alopecia universalis (i.e. total lack of hair, anywhere) and raised in an extremely abusive family, yet determined to graduate from college, get married and live a happy life. Last I heard, she was doing it, too. I've seen patients overcome Satanic torture and abuse and end up happy, healthy, and loving people. If Morrie Schwartz could be happy, so can you. . .

Part II   MAKE TWO SOMEONES HAPPY
Chapter Seven. Selecting a Mate:

For most people being happy essentially means being happily married. Most people do marry at some point in their lives, and studies pretty clearly demonstrate that on the average married people (especially men) are happier and healthier than single ones. We marry someone we believe will make us happy, and if we're not happy, we tend to blame our spouses. For example, this is what often happens in a "mid-life crisis." As we noted earlier in this book, a mid-life crisis is at its heart an identity crisis, a profound uncertainty and dissatisfaction with who you are. It is akin to adolescence, the prototypical identity crisis, which is why forty-year-olds in a mid-life crisis run around acting like teenagers. But the mid-lifer often doesn't recognize this and looks elsewhere for the cause of his distress, most notably to his wife. "I married you so you'd make me happy," he figures. "If I'm not happy, it must be because you aren't doing your job." So he dumps her for another adolescent like himself, only to discover the problem was actually within himself all along, not with his wife.

This is the kind of logic many of us bring to matrimony, but it is, as we have already seen in another context, fallacious. You can't really make anybody happy but yourself and nobody can make you happy either. You have to make yourself happy, and if you're married, this means you have to make yourself happy with your chosen mate. But here's where Nature throws us a bit of a curve ball, at least in terms of how our society goes about the process of mate selection. Because we base marriage largely on romantic love, we are almost guaranteed to pick a mate who is quite different from ourselves and therefore more difficult to be happy with. Here's how the process works.

Falling in Love:

Throughout most of history, most societies have left mate selection in the wise and objective hands of the parents, not the prospective newlyweds. Wise in the ways of the world and not blinded by love's passions, parents chose sturdy, responsible and potentially prosperous mates for their offspring. They chose mates who would provide financial security and produce healthy children to help with the farm chores. Love, much less sex appeal, was not a prime consideration. Yet, remarkably enough, couples who met for the first time at the altar learned over the years to love and cherish each other. The fact that divorce was not an option is obviously relevant here. You couldn't check out, so you could either learn to love your spouse or live a lifetime in misery. The point is, you can learn to love someone and learn how to be happy with someone, and many people did so.

Our modern society does courtship and marriage quite differently, for better or for worse. We fall in love. (Which may contribute significantly to the fact that we have the highest divorce rate in all history.)

Falling in love is a curious and complicated phenomenon about which much remains a mystery. We don't really know why we fall in love at all, much less why we fall in love with one person and not another. We do know that much of the driving force behind the in-love experience comes down to pure sexual attraction, though it's difficult to say exactly what it is that turns you on about a particular individual. It's not just good looks, in whatever way looks "good" to you. You may recognize that someone is drop-dead gorgeous yet not be physically attracted to her or at all prone to fall in love with her. And it's not just sexy behavior, either, though having a few good moves can more than compensate for relatively plain facial features or a less than stunning figure. In any case, sexual desire is clearly part of the in-love equation, perhaps reflecting Nature's profound interest in perpetuating the species and finding the best possible genes to pass on. It may even be that our sexual preferences reflect some deeper biological intelligence leading us to select a good reproductive partner. Sexual attraction alone, however, is not very likely to produce wise choices for a psychological match-up. Lust may make the world go 'round, but it may also cause it to wobble on its axis a bit. Unfortunately, the psychological side of falling in love is even more complicated and difficult to comprehend than the biological side and even more prone to lead us into troublesome relationships.

It appears that much of what underlies falling in

love is an effort to gratify unmet infantile dependency needs. That is, human infants are utterly dependent on their parents for their very survival. They must be fed, sheltered from the cold, protected from predators, moved to safe locations and perhaps cleaned and groomed a bit, or they will die. They also require love and without it will die psychologically if not physically. Thus, human infants form a powerful psychological, even biological bond with their mother or other primary caretakers. Infants raised without attention and affection from their caregivers have a high mortality rate. The ones who do survive will typically suffer gross impairment in their ability to bond with and relate to others. No parent, of course, is able to provide perfect love or meet all of a child's emotional needs. What we missed out on as infants we try to recoup as adults, by recreating the maternal bond in a marital relationship. Thus, in a way, we fall in love with someone who seems to us (at an unconscious level) a perfect loving mother or father, someone who will meet all our emotional needs, make us feel wonderful about ourselves and always "be there" for us. So, naturally we tend to fall in love with someone who resembles our real mother or father in some important way. "I want a girl just like the girl who married dear old Dad" says the old song. But someone like Mom may not be a very good choice for you, even if she was for the old man. This is even more true if Mom had a lot of psychological problems or was unable to relate effectively to her babies.

Perhaps the best example of this situation is seen in the daughters of alcoholic fathers. Alcoholic men tend to be emotionally needy and immature, as well as thoroughly self-absorbed. They are too busy trying to nurture themselves, looking for happiness at the bottom of a bottle, to do much in the way of fathering or nurturing their children. Thus, the daughters of alcoholics tend to grow up lacking the fatherly love they need to feel "special" and secure. When they go out in search of a mate these women are still in need of being "Daddy's Little Girl," and unconsciously they are looking for a substitute father. So they fall in love with men who look to them like fathers, which is to say, alcoholics. Often these men are much older than they and tend to be distant, unemotional, even abusive. Daughters of alcoholic men are notorious for marrying alcoholics because that's what a Daddy looks like to them, and therefore that's who they are programmed to be drawn to by their childhood experiences. My personal record is a patient who married eight alcoholics in a row. Further, it's hard to fight this tendency because it's largely unconscious. And it isn't the alcoholism per se that attracts them; it's the behavior pattern and way of relating. Children of alcoholics are often co-dependent because they grow up taking care of their fathers. They need to be needed and fall easily into caretaking relationships, which is just what the alcoholic is looking for. The worst drinker of the eight men noted above never drank during their courtship, at least not when he was going to see her. She picked him anyway.

At a less dramatic level, whatever problems your parent had, and whatever difficulties in relating to the opposite sex are likely to show up in your spouse. You grew up learning to act the way Mom thought a woman (or man) should act. You learned to relate to men by relating to Mom's choice in men, i.e. your Dad. Thus, you're programmed to select a mate who resembles your father (mother, for men) and to relate as your mother did to your father. People are amazed to find they've created a marriage remarkably similar to that of their parents, with exactly the same kinds of problems. As we've seen, however, this is almost predictable given the way we are unconsciously programmed. By the way, trying to avoid this outcome by selecting someone opposite to your other-sex parent isn't all that likely to result in a successful match either. It simply trades one problem for its opposite. For example, you might avoid marrying a spendthrift like your Mom only to end up with a tightwad like your Dad, which is just as hard to deal with.

Opposites Attract:

Which brings us to another way of looking at the problem of mate selection: opposites attract. This is an old cliche, recently re-popularized in John Gray's nicely written Mars/Venus books. Unfortunately, in many ways, it turns out to be true. In physics a strong negative charge and a strong positive charge attract each other, and their difference creates an electrical current. With people it's very much the same. The "spark" between two lovers comes in large measure from the opposite qualities which draw them together. Of course, sometimes there's too much electricity between them, and a violent thunder storm may be the result.

It's as if each of us is trying to complete himself or herself psychologically and is therefore drawn to possess what he or she lacks. Most obviously, male attracts female and vice versa. A man lacking in all feminine attributes has no refinement, no sensitivity, no aesthetic sensibility, no gentleness. He is a brute, not a "gentleman." On the other hand, a woman with no masculine qualities lacks ambition, firmness of will, assertiveness and perhaps even playfulness. We not only need each other, we need to be like each other in order to be fully developed human beings. We try to gain what we lack in our own masculinity or femininity by securing a mate of the opposite sex. Even gay couples often tend to pair up with one being more masculine, the other feminine. (Incidentally, becoming parents can assist us greatly in developing the opposite side of our sexuality. Fathers must learn to be gentle and nurturing with their babies, while mothers must learn to be firm and disciplinary with their children. Some men are absolutely phobic about babies and won't take care of their infants for fear of making a mistake or looking unmasculine. These misguided macho men are blowing a wonderful opportunity to develop the feminine ability to nurture, become true gentlemen and form a bond with their offspring which will greatly facilitate the discipline required as they mature.)

Opposites attract in other ways as well. For example, an extravert and an introvert will be drawn to each other magnetically. Type A's find Type B's, and good girls find bad boys utterly irresistible, much to the chagrin of their mothers. Then the fun begins. How they deal with their oppositeness will determine the success or failure and the happiness of the marriage. Opposites attract and marry, only to discover they are bonded to an alien creature! Venus falls in love with Mars, but when the honeymoon is over she may find it hard to live with his warrior mentality. A spendthrift and a tightwad will pick each other out of a crowd, fall in love, marry, then fight about money. When you marry your opposite, you still don't possess that opposite quality in yourself, and it is therefore still foreign and uncomfortable to you. Couples handle these differences in many ways, some leading to enhanced personal growth and marital happiness, others to conflict, misery and divorce. Marriage offers the opportunity for a kind of psychotherapeutic experience or for disaster, depending on how couples react to their differences. Let's see what does and doesn't work.

The problem does not present itself at first because of the idealizing aspect of being in love. When you're in love you think your mate is Sir

Lancelot, the perfect knight in shining armor, or Guinevere, a princess from an old fairly tale. You are married to the most beautiful, most wonderful, most loving person in the world, who can do no wrong and who makes you feel wonderful about yourself. After all, you must be a pretty special guy to have caught such a spectacular bride. Eventually, though, reality sets in and you begin to fall out of love, and to see your spouse as she or he truly is. Sir Lancelot would not leave the bathroom in the condition your husband does or leave his bloody swords lying around for you to pick up. Guinevere wouldn't be so grouchy and nagging about your mead-hall carousing with the other knights, no matter what her hormones were doing. It turns out you're married to a real human being, not a fantasy, a flawed, fallible and sometimes indecipherable person. Like you. Many people become very angry and disillusioned at this realization. They either decide they've made an awful mistake and leave, or they try to reshape the spouse into the desired fantasy, or they simply get angry and belligerent and hateful. It is to some extent an ego thing: how can I be a perfect husband if you won't be a perfect wife? For that matter, how could a smart guy like me have made such a foolish choice? Our Medieval ancestors, who more or less invented Romance, had sense enough to keep it at a fantasy level, by loving "pure and chaste from afar" and separating infatuation from marriage. A knight carried into battle the symbol of another lady, not his wife or wife-to-be. But we make our marriages around the in-love experience and end up having to deal with a real mate, and therefore, with our real selves. Lancelot and Guinevere broke the rules by consummating their romantic affair. Guinevere, you'll recall, was married to King Arthur, and her love for Lance was supposed to be only a pure, Platonic ideal. It's a lot harder to keep on loving someone when you have to deal day to day with the real person instead of a fantasy. But once you begin to fall out of love, the real work of making a marriage begins.

If I seem to be pretty negative, critical, even fatalistic about the in-love phenomenon, let me reassure you that I am not. I love being in love, same as anybody. On a good day I might fall in love three or four times. It's just that a fantasy trip isn't a very firm foundation on which to construct a marriage. I'm also not saying you can't hang on to any of the warm in- love feelings you begin the marriage with, though it may take a little effort and perhaps ingenuity at times.

Say, for what were hot-tubs meant or try some courting in a tent. You can still have a rush of in-love feelings when you see your mate especially well done-up for a party, when he sends you flowers for Valentine's, as you stroll hand-in-hand along a moonlit beach. Sex occasionally helps. (In fact, you need to be careful who you regularly have sex with, since "making love" does engender feelings of love. You can end up thinking you love someone when you merely love having sex with them.) But you can't sustain the feelings of being in love over time, all the time. Fortunately, love isn't just a matter of feelings, but of behavior, attitude, and commitment.

Cohabitation:

While we're looking at the process of selecting a mate, it's worth commenting on the modern strategy of cohabitation as a means of testing whether two people are a good match. This isn't really a new strategy, but our society has recently adopted it pretty much wholesale, and with fairly widespread approval. The idea is that when you fall in love with somebody, the two of you should move in together and try living as if married for a while. See if you can put up with each other for days at a time instead of just on weekend nights. See if you have little habits or traits that you just can't tolerate in each other. See if you're "compatible." If not, you can split up without all the legal and financial hassles of a divorce, perhaps even with reduced psychological distress. It's really quite a sensible notion and only has one thing wrong with it: Turns out it doesn't work. In fact, research now shows that couples who cohabitate before marrying have a much higher rate of divorce than couples who don't live together before exchanging vows. How can we explain this counterintuitive result?

There are probably several factors working to produce this outcome. Perhaps couples who cohabitate take too casual a view of marriage in the first place. They pop in and out of relationships with little thought for the long run. Perhaps they don't try hard enough to make the relationship work, knowing they can easily dissolve it. Perhaps their decision to live together instead of wedding indicates a subconscious scepticism about the strength of the relationship. In any case, they simply don't have the firm commitment necessary to make any marriage survive the hard times that will inevitably occur. When the going gets tough, they simply get going. Besides, it just isn't a realistic trial of the relationship. Living together is much easier than being married, because it's temporary, non-binding, just for fun. I've seen couples live together harmoniously as lovebirds for years, then fight like gamecocks as soon as the knot is tied. After all, when you're truly married, little things take on tremendous importance. You're playing for keeps now! It's a shame it's turned out this way, but as a strategy for finding a good mate and making a happy marriage, cohabitation has been a bust.

Considering what we've just said about how sex affects relationships and about the negative results of our societal experiment with cohabitation, I think young people should be advised to take it more slowly in their relationships than has become the norm today. Many single people assume they should become sexually involved with new partners by the third or fourth date (if not the first.) They seem to adopt a strategy of sleeping with a lot of folks, then sorting out who they like enough to marry. This is not only risky in terms of venereal diseases, it also is a poor way of selecting a mate. It places sex too much at the center of relationships, before there is any real knowledge of each other as persons. It becomes hard to know if it is a good relationship or just good sex. Once the line is crossed and a couple become sexually intimate, they rarely turn back to a Platonic relationship. Thus, I think it is a good idea to hold off until you really know and value and respect each other as persons. This makes sex the natural product of a loving relationship, an expression of a love that truly exists, rather than the whole basis for the relationship. Women reading this may fear that they will seem prudish or lose a good potential mate if they insist on waiting to become sexual. I understand the fear, but I think it is unfounded. A man who truly respects you will understand your concerns and will wait. He may become impatient or frustrated, but he'll hang in there. In fact, he'll probably try courting you more intensely– more flowers, nicer restaurants, etc. If he doesn't, you'll only have lost a guy who just wanted to use you. There's some truth in the old adage that you won't buy the whole cow if you're already getting the milk for free.

Marrying in Hopes He'll Change:

Before leaving the topic of mate selection, we should mention a particularly disastrous strategy for finding your life's partner. This is to select one you believe has the potential to be what you desire, marry him, then change him to suit your needs. Many people, especially women, I think, adopt this strategy, perhaps out of desperation, perhaps in the mistaken belief that love will conquer all or that they have the power to transform frogs into princes. This strategy runs dead up against what we've found to be true elsewhere in this work, namely that **you can change only one human being on earth, and that's yourself.** Certainly people change after the wedding, but it's often for the worst. Indeed, a cynic might compare marriage to brain damage, where the rule of thumb is that a brain injury makes you the way you always were, only more so. If a man is inconsiderate of you before the wedding, when he's courting you and presumably on his best behavior, after the honeymoon is over he's likely to neglect you altogether. If your girlfriend seems a bit dependent and whiney, she's likely to make a wife who nags and bitches constantly. If you can't live with your fiancé the way he is, dump him now and keep on looking. As a husband he is likely to be much worse.

Expectations for Married Life:
Having selected what they believe to be a perfect mate, most people enter married life expecting a blissful, intimate, loving and relaxed relationship. Most people get this for a while; it's called the Honeymoon. Some people get this for the majority of their married lives, but not without effort. The range of outcomes is obviously pretty broad. I saw a lady whose husband had at least one affair on their

honeymoon. I've seen couples who never had a real argument, although some of them desperately needed to have a good fight, clear the air and get something resolved. Some marriages are easy, others hard. Some last only a few months, others for many decades. Picking the right partner obviously helps a lot, but it is by no means enough. Work and commitment are required. I find that many people enter marriage with grossly unrealistic expectations for married life and for their spouses's behavior. Let's take a brief look at what one should realistically expect.

Expect there to be differences between you and your mate. We've already seen how opposites attract, so differences should be expected. And there's an infinite number of ways in which people can differ from each other. You may expect that your mate will naturally see and do things your way (being as this is the *right* way.) Forget it. You've got an internal blueprint showing how a marriage should be conducted, how a wife should act and what a husband should do. So does your partner. The trouble is, there are two different sets of plans. I think the husband should sleep on the left side of the bed, but my wife is just as sure this side is divinely ordained for the wife. Every one of these differences must be dealt with. Expect to have conflict and differences of perception. Forget about good and bad, and work out a mutually acceptable modus vivendi. Expect to lose some of these battles. Further, it is not realistic to expect your mate to fit smoothly into your family and its lifestyle on an instantaneous basis. It's likely to take time to learn how your family does things. Your new mate may not like or be liked by all your family, either. After all, most families have blood relatives who grew up together and hate each other.

Some people expect always to get what they want and need in marriage. Don't. There are bound to be some disappointments, if only because no one person can meet all your needs. Besides, your partner has needs of her own, and some will likely conflict with yours. Some people believe that if someone truly loves you they will anticipate your every need without having to be told. This is nonsense. Even true love doesn't make you a mind-reader. Likewise, some people believe that if their spouse truly loves them and clearly understands their viewpoint, they will always agree with them. Bunk. Loving couples are bound to disagree on all kinds of things, and this does not indicate a lack of love. For one thing, you're bound to be wrong occasionally. Do you want your mate to agree with you anyway? Similarly, I can truly understand and respect your opinion, but have a differing opinion of my own.

Some people expect their marriage partner to enjoy doing all the same hobbies, going to the same events, eating the same foods. While you're likely to develop some common interests and at least learn to tolerate each others' interests, don't expect ever to share all of them.

It is not realistic to expect your spouse to change

just because you desire it. It is even less realistic to believe that you can change your mate. It is terribly unrealistic to expect never to have to change yourself. Indeed, marriage will probably change you as much as anything else in your life, hopefully for the better.

Expect to fall out of love. Infatuation is too much a fantasy trip to survive the practical realities of everyday married life. You *can* realistically expect to fall back into love now and again, especially if you work at it a bit. Don't expect to have sex whenever you want or for it always to be passionate or tender or romantic or for your partner to desire all the same things that turn you on. Be prepared to compromise, learn something new, be happy with what you've got.

Don't expect never to argue or disagree with your spouse. Conflict is a part of every long-term relationship. How you resolve it is the key to a happy marriage. I've seen couples who had an argument and assumed the marriage was over. Not so. Expect to abandon this sort of all or nothing, black or white thinking; marital relationships contain too many shades of gray.

Expect things to change and then change some more. People change over time, circumstances change, feelings change. Expect to have to adapt to these changes and expect it to be hard some times.

Expect to be married to this person for the rest of your life. Without this expectation and the commitment that goes with it, you may as well head for the lawyer's office now.

Expect to be loved and accepted as perhaps never before in your life. Expect to be able to feel good about yourself. **Expect to be happy– but not all the time. And expect to have to work at it.**

Chapter Eight. Resolving Marital Differences
Resolving Marital Differences:

Trying to fix or correct your spouse won't work. We've already noted that you cannot change another human being. Thus, the enterprise is doomed to failure from the start. Further, most people don't like being "fixed," especially by their mates, and will actively resist change or transformation. Actually, there is nothing in your wedding vows or marriage contract that entitles you to criticize your mate, and most people don't like being criticized at all. When you love someone, you accept him or her as is- good, bad, and ugly (as we all are.) Trying to change your spouse clearly implies that he is not acceptable to you as is. That means you don't love him. Thus, your best-intentioned efforts to fix or improve your spouse will often be perceived as unloving and rejecting, rather than helpful, and will be stubbornly resisted. If anything, your spouse may become even more solidly entrenched in her position. She may jolly well turn the tables as well, and try to fix you!

This way of dealing with the differences in a marriage can lead to a wild runaway process in which both parties become less healthy and the marriage blows violently apart. In effect, each spouse declares "Your way of being is wrong and mine is right; I will over-correct for your error by becoming even more strongly the way I am– the Right Way." The other naturally counters with the same message and maneuver. They react to each other by becoming more and more polarized, more and more extreme, farther and farther apart. Instead of growing and developing in a healthy way they become stereotyped, eventually turning almost into caricatures of themselves. They become so polarized that compromise is impossible.

Take the spendthrift and the tightwad. To her, money is a source of security. She feels very much threatened by her husband's spending, if not personally offended as well. Her anxious response may be to save even more than usual, as an over-correction to his profligate ways. To him, money is a source of gratification and independence, pleasure and power. He is threatened by her meanness and feels that she is holding out on him and trying to tell him what to do. He rebels and spends more wildly than ever. This pattern of mutual over-reaction can escalate to wild proportions. I saw a couple in which the wife was squirreling away money in every possible way, watering down the milk, passing off cheap hamburger as ground sirloin, even falsifying the checkbook to hide money from her husband. He in turn bought a fifteen-thousand dollar bass boat he couldn't afford, just to show her he could do it. In fact, the poor guy was afraid of water and didn't swim, ski or fish; the boat never saw a lake. Pretty clearly, this is not a healthy way to resolve basic differences in attitudes about finances. Nor a cheap one.

An even more destructive example of this dysfunctional way of dealing with opposite qualities in marriage is often seen in parenting disputes. All parental activities may be roughly categorized as either nurturing or disciplinary in nature. Nurturing involves taking care of children, showing them affection, playing with them. Discipline involves teaching children how to behave, often through the use of rewards and punishments or perhaps by lecturing (often the worst punishment of all.) All children require both nurturing and discipline to develop normally, hopefully delivered in a responsible balance and by both parents. Both discipline and nurturing are acts of love, done in the best interests of the child. This is why children do not react with hatred to appropriate discipline. Indeed, they generally become not only more compliant, but more affectionate when appropriately disciplined. But again, natural styles vary and opposites will tend to attract each other. It's common, then, that one parent will naturally be more prone to discipline, the other to nurture, even in handling the same exact situation. Inability to reconcile these opposite tendencies will not only create marital strife, but they may also have disastrous consequences for the children. One parent, let's say the Mom, feels the child's misbehavior is an indication of low self-esteem and reflects a need for more attention. The other parent, Dad in this case, feels the child is simply rebellious and needs "to have his butt tore up." Mom sees Dad's solution to the problem as ill-advised, unloving, and perhaps calculated to make matters worse by further lowering the child's self-esteem. So she decides to make up for his harshness by being extra loving and nurturing. Dad sees this and feels she's coddling their little criminal. He resolves to over-correct for this by becoming even more punitive. Soon, Mom and Dad are arguing with each other and the rift between them provides fertile ground for manipulation on the part of the child. Indeed, it aligns the child and his mother in an inappropriate and dangerous alliance against the father, threatening the stability of the entire family. Meanwhile, the parents are becoming increasingly polarized and extreme in their handling of the child, as they react to each other. Pretty soon Mom is spoiling the child rotten and Dad is outright abusing him. Both styles constitute bad parenting and can have serious deleterious consequences for the child, as well as destroying the marriage– which isn't good for any of them.

How can this kind of marital dispute be resolved? In the parenting example, several options are available. One is for the parents to get together, realize their children need balanced and reasonable parenting, and to discipline appropriately while also giving more attention to the child's *good* behavior and to his needs for affection. Another is to seek outside help and agree to follow the advice of a qualified, impartial consultant. This could be a counselor, pediatrician, grandparent, even a friend. Or they could simply agree to disagree and let one parent handle it his way for three weeks, then yield to the other's approach for three weeks. After six weeks of these two "experiments in parenting" they would examine and compare the results and then decide on an appropriate course of action. Any of these methods would resolve the dispute and provide a unified approach to parenting. Both parties would feel respected and their authority maintained.

Family therapists often deal with this kind of dispute with a fascinating and paradoxical strategy: they have the couple switch sides for a while. The nurturing parent is instructed to be the tough guy for a while, to lay down the law and impose consequences for misconduct as firmly as possible. The disciplinary parent is to back off and be a nice guy, spending time with the child in a playful and affectionate manner. This suggestion usually meets with astonishment and resistance from the parents, but if followed faithfully the results can be dramatically beneficial. The child receives a balanced mix of nurturing and discipline, meeting his needs, only now they're coming from the "wrong" parent. This keeps the child guessing (always a good idea) and may force her to see her parents in a different light. Who could have imagined that Dad could be so sweet and fun or Mom so tough! The parents, meanwhile, begin to experience and appreciate each other's way of seeing and doing things, seeing each other in a new light as well. Each grows as a person and a parent, becoming more capable and comfortable in both nurturing and discipline. They find it much easier to coordinate their functioning as a parental team and are better able to provide flexible, well-balanced responses to the child's needs. They are no longer so opposite, each being more like the other and both being more moderate. There is less disagreement and disputes are more easily resolved when they do arise.

A Model for Conflict Resolution in Marriage:
The foregoing discussions about parenting styles leads us to a general model for a positive, functional approach to resolution of marital differences. In dysfunctional marriages, the spouses try to change each other, becoming more polarized, stereotyped and entrenched in their opposite ways. In successful marriages, the spouses fix their own behavior, learning from each other, growing towards each other and meeting in the middle where balance is more easily achieved. Think of a seesaw and how hard it is to keep it balanced with both kids far out on the ends, as opposed to sitting nearer the fulcrum at the middle. **The model sequence for resolving marital differences is this: Understand, Accept, Appreciate and Emulate.**
Step One. Understanding. It is an unfortunate fact of human nature that simple mis-communication tends to produce conflict and animosity. We tend to assume that the other is acting in bad faith and is either evil (malicious, ill-intended) or incompetent (stupid, crazy.) We react accordingly. Many marital disputes reflect a simple, basic misunderstanding of the other's position and can be resolved by good,

clear communication. Often this occurs when there is no verbal communication and we are forced to rely on nonverbal messages instead. Nonverbal messages are hidden in our behavior, in *how* we say things. This includes our posture, tone of voice, gestures, timing, all of which can qualify the meaning of our words. Nonverbal messages are an inevitable aspect of *all* communication because all behavior says something and it is impossible *not* to behave. To say anything, you must say it in some way, and that way says something about how you feel, even if you choose to do it in print. Nonverbal messages actually have a stronger emotional impact than do verbal messages, but they are also much less clear and more subject to different interpretations. It is at the nonverbal level that we communicate how we feel about each other, that define, in effect, the nature of our relationships. For example, a guy goes into a bar and sits down next to a gorgeous girl. He declares it a lovely day to frolic in the park, but she replies that it looks like rain to her. This pair isn't talking about the weather, but negotiating about the nature of their potential relationship– at the nonverbal level. He's not upset about the negative weather forecast, but may be hurt she's rained on his parade.

It is easy to mis-communicate at the nonverbal level, and such misunderstandings can heavily impact our relationships. In the absence of sufficient clear verbal communication, we may mis- or over-interpret each other's behavior. For example, I once saw a woman who was on the verge of filing for divorce, swearing her husband didn't love her. She knew this because he was chronically tardy and resistant in carrying out the trash. To him this was simply an unpleasant chore he sought to avoid as long as possible. He'd procrastinate, make excuses, or simply "forget." But unbeknownst to him, to his wife carrying out the trash was a crucially important way a husband shows his love for his wife. She had evidently been impressed by her father's love for her mother, of which the trash chore, for some bizarre reason, was highly symbolic. Unfortunately, she'd never told her husband the meaning this behavior had for her, apparently assuming this to be a universal symbol of undying love. Thus, every time he delayed or forgot the trash, he was communicating to her his lack of love. She was devastated every Sunday and Wednesday. Once he understood what it meant to her, he was happy to take out the trash and did so quite faithfully, much to her delight. The marriage was saved and the kitchen smelled better, and all at no cost. The cure for mis-communication, especially the misinterpretation of nonverbal messages, is clear, direct verbal communication.

Similarly, a spouse's tight-fistedness with money is a lot easier to tolerate when one comes to realize that it is a way to meet a basic security need and does not reflect simply stinginess, meanness, or a desire to control. A husband's tendency to withdraw to the privacy of his office may be experienced by his wife as a rejection and abandonment. She may be so highly threatened that she responds by pursuing him and trying to engage him in dialogue, even if it means provoking a fight. He, in turn, may perceive this not as an attempt to restore intimacy, but as an attack or intrusion on his personal space. He may feel threatened, pressured, and trapped. Both will be better able to deal with this problem if she understands he needs time alone and he understands she needs time together. Neither is trying to hurt or reject, they simply have conflicting but legitimate needs.

Some couples are so obsessed with proving the other wrong that they don't really listen to each other's position. Each listens only well enough to compose his own rebuttal. It is not uncommon in my experience to see marital disputes simply vanish entirely once each understands accurately what the other is trying to say. Towards this end I will sometimes give each spouse in therapy five or ten *uninterrupted* minutes to have their say, after which the other may respond only when they have restated their spouses's views to the other's satisfaction. Then he or she can take a turn at expressing their own position. Many report this to be the first time in their marriage they have felt truly understood. Often it turns out they really weren't that far apart in the first place. In any case, it is a lot easier to accept and deal with your partner's alien way of being, once you clearly understand what it is.

Step Two. Acceptance. The next step in resolving

marital differences is acceptance. This is the way your spouse is. This is reality. Like it or not, rational or not, whatever you thought you were marrying, this is the reality of the person to whom you are actually married. You can't deny reality and you can't change it. **You can't fix your spouse or force him to fix himself.** You must accept your mate as is, which is a fairly good definition of love and something we all need from our relationships. Then you can begin trying to make yourself happy with this person.

This is not an easy process. It involves letting go of a very powerful fantasy and settling for a less-than-perfect reality. It means a change in self-concept as well, since your mate's not being a Princess means you aren't a Prince either. Many people become furious at their spouses for not being the Ideal Mate they thought they had married. Accepting your spouse as is involves a kind of forgiveness. Forgiveness, in effect, for being human. It involves a decision to see the other as is and be happy with that, to decide your mate is not perfect, but good enough. **That's why love is an act of will, not just of emotion.**

Bonnie Raitt describes this very nicely in her song "Good Enough." The song begins with the singer's mother wondering if her new boyfriend is "good enough" for her daughter. The daughter, meanwhile, is wondering if she's good enough for him! And both of them worry if their love-making is good enough for the other. Much later, as the relationship has solidified and matured, she notes, "It's strange how time's gone by since the day we fell in love; and still sometimes we have to ask ourselves is it good enough." But "Time," she concludes, "is bound to make us see, just how good 'good enough' can be." Remembering our discussion about the "good enough mother" and self-esteem being based on seeing oneself as good enough too, we see that these early childhood developments lay the foundation for adult-to-adult relationships that are also "good enough." "Good enough" isn't perfect but it is good enough to be happy with for a lifetime. And that kind of acceptance of your mate is an essential step in learning to be happy with her.

Step Three. Appreciation. Accepting your spouse's differences from you and deciding he is still ok is good enough to achieve a fairly comfortable level of marital adjustment. But if you really want to maximize your marriage and get all marriage has to offer, it is necessary to go farther. **Beyond mere acceptance is appreciation or learning to value the ways in which your mate differs from you.** This means seeing the difference as a potential asset rather than a liability, an opportunity to be treasured rather than annoyance to be tolerated. In this regard, it is helpful to see the difference as a difference in values, not just character traits. Each spouse, then, is seen to represent or uphold something to be respected and valued, even though it is different. Your spouse's way of being or of behaving is seen as a proper, legitimate and useful alternative to your own. It's not necessarily better or worse, just different. This means the two of you have more options available to you than if you agreed on everything. With two ways to perceive a situation, two strategies for problem solving, two approaches to the business of living, you double your chances of finding an optimal way to deal with any given circumstances you may confront. Indeed, one could argue that if you and your spouse saw everything the same way, one of you would be redundant and disposable. Of course, this viewpoint will only work if you truly learn to value your partner's different outlooks and figure out a way to coordinate them with your own. Instead of trying to establish that your way is right and your spouse's wrong, you respect each other's different values and try to determine what value is more important and will work out better in this particular situation.

Again, discipline and nurturing are both valuable aspects of a loving parental relationship, but what does *this* child need at *this* moment to help her grow and develop properly? Does she need understanding and affection or does she need to be grounded? If we respect and value each other's opinions and methods we can decide based on what is likely to work better, instead of getting into a destructive power struggle.

We may even learn something in the process. We may discover better ways of parenting, for example, but even more, we may begin to see how it feels to be the other. This is one way marriage can help you grow as a person. If I agree to try discipline with our child, your way, even though this feels wrong or unnatural to me, I begin to act like a disciplinarian and to think and feel like a disciplinarian. I become, to some degree, a disciplinary kind of person and I begin to see myself as a different person and become comfortable with this new me. I have then grown as a person, developing a disciplinary counterbalance to my naturally sweet, nurturing self. I have more options within myself and can better coordinate and balance my activities with those of my spouse. This is step four.

Step Four. Emulation. If I have accepted and then learned to value and appreciate my mate's way of being, then isn't it natural to want to become at least somewhat that way myself? If this is a good, though different way to act, wouldn't I be a better person, in some measure, if I could learn to act that way also? Beyond appreciation, then, is emulation, a more or less conscious decision to become more like your spouse. This is where real personal growth occurs in a marriage and how marriage can become a kind of automatic, built-in psychotherapy. It is also where a true and fundamental resolution of marital differences can occur. If I become more like you, then we're not so opposite anymore, especially if you also learn to appreciate and emulate me. In good marriages this is what tends to occur. In fact, it turns out that the process, once begun, tends to feed on itself. Here's how it works.

One spouse decides to quit fighting reality, quit trying to change her mate, and instead to accept him as he is. She comes to see that in some ways it's actually good and valuable to be the way her husband is. She sets out to learn how to do it herself. Seeing the change, her husband no longer feels attacked or criticized, so he stops being defensive and argumentative. Perhaps for the first time he feels totally accepted, even respected, valued and appreciated for being himself. Which is to say, he feels loved. He no longer feels the need to justify himself or denigrate his wife or prove her wrong. He is gratified and appreciative of his wife and can look more objectively at the situation. He begins to notice that her way of doing things is also valuable and useful. He decides to become more like her. Her acceptance and valuing of him has freed him to grow and develop in her direction. Instead of becoming more polarized and entrenched in their differences, they become more alike and grow closer together. Neither has lost anything of himself, but both have become better balanced as individuals. This makes it easier to achieve balance in their relationship because they aren't way out at the extremes of behavior.

For an example, let's return to the tightwad and the spendthrift. If he can stop feeling threatened and controlled by her frugality, he may begin to realize that it's actually advantageous to have someone in the family who can put a little something aside for the future. "You know," he says to himself, "my wife is really good at saving money, and that's a good thing. We'd never have been able to get that big-screen television if she hadn't saved up for it. I love to spend money, but Lord knows I could never have gotten that set if I'd had to do it on my own. In fact, I'd like to be able to save like she does. By Gosh, I'm gonna start putting aside some of the raise I just got. I'll never really miss it, and with both of us saving we might just be able to add on to the house some day."

His wife sees her husband regularly adding to the savings account and breathes a sigh of relief. Not only has he quit spending impulsively and quit griping about her "penny-pinching" ways, but he's actually become a partner in her savings plan. She feels accepted and appreciated and she, in turn, appreciates her husband's willingness to change and help her meet her needs. "This is great," she says. "I don't have to do all the saving because my husband is helping. Think of all we can put aside together. Meanwhile, he's got a point, too. We can't just live for the future. We work hard and should have a little something to show for it now. In fact, since our future looks more secure now, I'll splurge a little and make a dinner reservation at that fancy place he's been dying to try." This makes him feel accepted, appreciated and loved. The money fight is over, retirement is more secure and each feels appreciated and valued now. Both spouses come out winners. It is paradoxical, but in learning to be more like your spouse, you help your mate become more like you as well.

The Most Common Marital Conflicts:

It is axiomatic amongst family therapists that there is a battle in *every* marriage, and in a very real sense this is true. Each of us comes into a marriage with a sort of blueprint for how to construct a proper marital relationship. This blueprint is partly conscious and partly unconscious, a set of assumptions based largely on what you grew up with and observed in your parents' marriage. These plans specify how a husband should act, how a wife should act and how they should relate to each other, to in-laws, to kids, to the rest of the world. Each of us then sets about building our new home according to the blueprints. The trouble is, our spouse has a different set of plans, having grown up observing a different marital relationship. So the battle is on, not so much to control each other as to control the definition of the relationship itself. Are we going to build our home using your set of blueprints or my set, i.e. your way or the right way?

Imagine the chaos that ensues from trying to construct a home with two sets of plans. The back door opens into empty space (no deck) and there's a toilet and sink in the living room (which is the bathroom on your set of plans.)

For most couples no amount of arguing will produce an agreement to use one of these sets of blueprints and reject the other. And, since each marriage is in some ways unique, chances are good that neither set of plans will be exactly right for them. Thus, I tell the couples I work with to be ready to chuck both of their preconceived ideas of how a marriage should operate and develop a new model. This may include some elements from each spouse's family background and some entirely new ones. The important thing is to agree that this is the way we're going to run *our* marriage, however our parents ran theirs.

There are many issues that need to be resolved in a new marriage, but the following seem to be the most common problem areas.

Power:

Power or decision-making is often the first, last, and major area of conflict. The question here is who is going to decide how we conduct our marriage and run our home. Do we have equal authority or is one of us the boss? Or perhaps you can tell me what to do in the kitchen while I control what happens in the yard. There are many ways to go, but the question must be resolved or a marriage collapses into anarchy, bickering and power plays. Our whole society is in the middle of a major transition on the issue of authority in a marriage, and couples are struggling with it in their own marriages. (Indeed, we seem to have troubles with authority issues in general, due perhaps to government duplicity in Vietnam, corruption in high office, and the misguided advice of do-gooder social scientists such as myself, who have over-emphasized individual needs and self-esteem over the welfare of society at large.) In effect we have two competing models of marriage, two radically different sets of rules, values, and expectations. Couples find themselves lost in between with no clear guidelines. Here's the breakdown:

The Traditional Model has been universally accepted and practiced in our society for thousands of years. It sets up what communications and systems theorists call a "complementary relationship." Husband and wife have different roles which complement each other. The husband is clearly defined as dominant and possessing the ultimate authority in the family. The wife is subordinate, submissive and supportive. He takes care of her, brings home the bacon and makes all major decisions. She cooks the bacon, takes care of the kids, and obeys his commands. Hers is the power to persuade– only.

This model has worked well for a long time and will still work, but only if *both* spouses fully agree with it. It has several advantages. Role definitions are very clear, and everyone knows what to do and what to expect. It is a very stable configuration for a relationship. In some ways it seems to "fit" biologically, with males being more powerful and aggressive, females more nurturing and submissive, as they are in most other mammals, including primates. It is enshrined in our religious traditions and writings and receives the support of the conservative religious community. It is how most of us were brought up and is therefore familiar and relatively comfortable, needing little clarification or indoctrination. It has largely weathered the test of time.

But the traditional model has disadvantages, too. It is pretty rigid and inflexible and so is relatively unable to adapt rapidly to changing circumstances. This reduces the marriage's survivability. Let's not forget what happened to the dinosaurs. They were superbly adapted to a very stable and uniform climate, in a world consisting of only one massive continent. There was little variation in the weather, the climate, the environment in general, and dinosaurs ruled the planet for 160 million years. Mammals evolved around the same time as the dinos but never got much bigger than a small dog or cat. But as the world changed, continents drifted apart and mountain ranges were thrust up, and dramatic variations in weather began to occur, the dinosaurs were too locked-in to change readily. They began to decline. When an asteroid exploded off the coast of Yucatan and *really* changed the environment, producing a couple years of nothing but winter, the dinosaurs died out. The runty little mammals crawled into their burrows and survived on nuts and roots and emerged to conquer the planet. They were flexible enough to adapt to change. The Traditional, complementary model of marriage may be our societal dinosaur, unable to adapt to the most rapidly changing times in all human history.

The Traditional model of marriage is also quite limiting in its rigid role definitions, locking individuals into behavior patterns which may be inefficient or inappropriate to their unique skills and attitudes. A traditional husband may barbeque, but he doesn't really cook, even if he can out-gourmet Julia Childs. A traditional wife doesn't handle the family's investments, even if Wall Street is begging her to lead the way to mutual prosperity. The traditional model allows males to be harsh, even abusive, while also placing the entire burden of decision-making on them. It's just not an efficient use of people's talents, as well as potentially demeaning or abusive.

The Modern Model of marriage is egalitarian, or, in Systems Theory terms, "symmetrical." The spouses are equal, with shared decision-making authority and balanced roles. Neither tells the other what to do; oftentimes both are employed; and chores are assigned with little regard for traditional gender-based roles (at least in theory.) The egalitarian marriage developed largely during the fifties and sixties in the United States, presumably spurred to a great extent by the changes brought about by World War II. While the boys were overseas killing each other, the girls took to the factories to make guns and bombs for them to do it with. Some of them were pretty good at it and didn't particularly want to quit and go back home when the boys returned after the War. And, sadly, there were fewer boys in any case. The girls liked the new freedom they'd discovered, the idea of being more than wives and mothers, the power that came from earning their own money. Further, changes in the post-war economy gradually reshaped the employment picture in our society. We had, and found we needed, more neat stuff than ever before. We also found that it took two wage-earners to afford the two-car family, the two-garage home and the televisions, dishwashers and microwaves inside the home. With husband and wife both working out-side the home, the structure of the family changed, and so did the model for marital relationships.

The egalitarian marriage has tremendous potential for liberating and actualizing both spouses, but especially wives. Talents formerly suppressed by gender-stereotyped roles are now more fully utilized. Both partners feel respected, share responsibility, make decisions. This model fits well with our democratic ideals and reflects a general movement towards the liberation of women in our society. After all, if you're bringing home half the bacon, it seems fair for you to help decide how to slice it.

There are, of course, drawbacks to the egalitarian model, just as with the traditional model. Because the two partners must stay equally balanced, this is a less stable configuration than the traditional marriage. Roles, duties, and expectations must all be negotiated and decided upon by each individual couple, and always by a consensus vote. There are few traditional guidelines or cultural norms for how to conduct such a relationship. There is no final authority, and decision-making may falter or lead to a power vacuum. Both spouses may be challenged to take on new and uncomfortable roles or duties, or to keep up with a spouse who is rapidly developing and growing. This may be good for you, but it can also be tiring and anxiety-producing. Power struggles erupt more frequently and more heatedly in the modern than the traditional marriage, and there is very little in the way of outside support systems when the relationship hits a crisis point. There's also a new area of conflict in most modern marriages that rarely occurred in the old. This is the conflict over whose career goals and demands has the higher priority. In the old days, if Dad got transferred, everybody packed up and moved with him to the new job. Or perhaps Dad decided to quit and take a different position. The wife and family supported him in his decision– and it was essentially *his* decision. But now, with both spouses typically working, conflicting career goals and needs become marital conflicts as well. What happens to the family if Mom gets a big promotion that requires her to move to Cleveland, but Dad has a stable pediatric practice back home in Miami? You can't just move a private practice without tremendous loss of income. On the other hand, if Mom turns down this transfer, she'll never get another chance to move into upper management and the big bucks available at that level. Whose career takes priority? Some couples try the long-distance commute and live in separate states, flying back and forth on weekends. From my experience, this is often the first step towards divorce court. But how does a couple make this kind of decision? In the egalitarian marriage, both careers are equally valued, and both have equal decision-making authority. This change in family authority patterns and in the parental roles associated with them may also be a contributor to the general breakdown of parental authority we've experienced in the last three decades.

Most of us were raised in families operating under the old, traditional model of marriage. We are more familiar with and comfortable with this type of relationship and may be shocked or offended to find our spouse has a different plan. This is especially true for men, most of whom grew up watching their fathers be in charge of their mothers. These men may simply assume they have the right, even the duty, to control their wives in any way they like. The result may be a marital conflict, a power struggle over the definition of the marriage. When a couple is arguing "over everything," this kind of power struggle underlies all the more specific issues. That's why seemingly trivial areas of disagreement rapidly escalate into full-scale warfare. It's not the thing itself but the symbolic value that counts. I don't object to taking out the trash; I object to your telling me to do so. The trash chore comes to symbolize power in the relationship (just as it came to symbolize love in another marriage we've looked at.) I've seen couples who argued viciously about absolutely everything in their relationship, with neither willing to concede even the most minor point for fear of losing a strategic advantage in the war. These guys can't even get help from a marriage counselor because they can't agree on who to see, when to make the appointments, whose insurance to file under, etc.

Many parenting disputes and most money battles are really power struggles at heart. It's not about how to discipline, it's about who gets to decide how to discipline. The issue isn't spending money, it's about who has the power to decide whether to spend it or not. There are many possible resolutions of this issue, but for marital harmony it must be resolved. And the resolution must be mutually satisfactory or the battle will continue, at least in covert, passive-aggressive resistance. Some couples will revert to the male-dominant, traditional model because at least it provides for clear lines of authority and role definitions. Some will divide authority across different areas, with the husband in charge of yards, cars, and vacations; the wife managing finances, food and children. Increasingly, the resolution is to adopt the egalitarian model of an equal partnership, with a total sharing of power. As a marriage counselor, I must say that I find this model most comfortable to work with. I also find that couples who learn to work within this model and relate as equals seem to have the happiest, most successful, and most fulfilling marriages. But it is not the easiest resolution to achieve, and it isn't a once and for all times problem solved. As family circumstances and the individuals within it change, the balance of power can change also, threatening the equality of the marital relationship. Many wives, for example, are dismayed to find that when they quit work to raise children, they suddenly lose all power in the marriage. Some husbands find the same when they are laid-off, disabled, or retired. Some changes in circumstances may *require* that one spouse take over control (e.g. the other is mentally incapacitated) although this may be threatening to both of them. Still, democracy and equality are the American Way, or at least the way we'd like ourselves to be, and the advantages of the modern, egalitarian marriage greatly outweigh the disadvantages in the long run. It just generally seems the most loving and respectful way to do business, especially marital business.

Couples who continue to battle for power have very unhappy marriages– or divorces. Incidentally, divorce typically doesn't resolve the power struggle either. It just shifts the battleground a bit. All that's left to fight over are kids and money, so that's what exes battle over. Finally, I can't resist mentioning a particularly bizarre way of failing to resolve power issues in marriage. I've seen couples wherein each insisted the other take charge and be the boss. They wanted not to assume but to abdicate power and responsibility. Predictably, these couples have a hard time getting anything accomplished. They don't get very far in therapy either. For the most part they sit quietly saying, "I don't know; what do *you* want to talk about?"

Intimacy:

Intimacy is the other major issue to be resolved in a marriage. We can define intimacy as "the sharing of emotionally-laden experiences." Thus, intimacy would include sexual closeness, but also the closeness and intense feelings a couple share at the birth of a child. It includes also grieving together over a lost loved one, even getting angry at each other. **Intimacy is a sharing of life's meaningful experiences together.** It is a revealing to the other of one's true self. It means exposing one's self to the other and being able to identify empathically with the other. It is essential and basic to what makes us human.

One must assume that anyone who marries is desirous of some kind of intimacy, unless the marriage is purely political or merely convenient (and excepting the shotgun marriage which is the penalty for intimacy already shared.) But intimacy comes in many varieties and degrees, and there is no guarantee that husband and wife want the same kind or the same amount or the same intensity of intimacy. He may be interested primarily in sexual intimacy, which psychologist Willard Harley lists as men's number one need in marriage (in the book *His Needs, Her Needs*). She's okay with sex but what she needs to feel close to her mate is affection and conversation– numbers one and two on Dr. Harley's list for women, but not in the top five for men. Or perhaps they have similar needs but their timing is different. He likes to make love at night, but she's a morning person who crashes at 8:30, just as he's getting fired up. He likes to talk after, she before. He wants to recount and rehash all the events of the day, while she's content with a brief chat on weekends. There's plenty of room for differences and disagreements, and disputes about intimacy tend to be especially painful and intense. They cut to the heart of who we are. Thus, learning to regulate their intimate relationship is a make-it or break-it issue for every married couple.

People feel comfortable with quite different levels of closeness. What to me is a comfortable distance for conversing with someone may feel too close, even intrusive to you. This is true of physical space but also of emotional intensity or degree of openness. If you walk into my office, sit in my lap and talk about your sex life, I may feel you've crossed my personal boundaries with neither invitation nor permission. I may feel intruded upon, even assaulted. On the other hand, if I roll my chair back into a remote corner, hide behind the desk and press up against the wall, you may find me a trifle remote, not to say rejecting and cold. Because this kind of nonverbal behavior communicates how we feel about each other, it defines our relationship in emotional terms. This can set up some highly charged and dysfunctional patterns of relating. Likewise, your refusal to reveal yourself to me, to talk of anything personal, to share your feelings, may, in a relationship supposedly defined as intimate, be interpreted as hostile and rejecting.

In most marriages one member of the couple will want more intimacy than the other. The other will be uncomfortable with too much closeness, perhaps even actually afraid of it. After all, it is only someone close to you who can truly hurt you personally. Becoming intimate is somewhat scary to everybody, and rightly so. The spouse who needs more intimacy will naturally approach the other, seeking a closer connection. This may be threatening to the mate, however, who now feels intruded upon or "too close for comfort." He (It's more likely the guy) backs off to a safe distance, physically and/or emotionally. This however is threatening to his wife, because it feels to her like an abandonment and rejection. So she pursues him and tries in some way to get him more involved with her. He feels attacked and backs off again. This kind of interaction can become an habitual and escalating cycle of distancing and pursuit. The harder she chases, the more desperately he withdraws, until finally she backs him into a corner and *forces* him to relate to her.

This can be downright dangerous. We are describing a relationship pattern which can generate very intense emotions, even leading to physical violence. In my experience people are most likely to experience panic attacks when they feel either abandoned or trapped. In the Distancer-Pursuer interaction the former feels trapped and the latter feels abandoned, so both can become extremely agitated. I've seen a number of these couples in which she finally cornered him and he slugged her, lashing out like a trapped animal. Moreover, this scenario can become a stable pattern of marital violence. This emotionally laden and physically violent interaction meets our definition of intimacy, because it involves a shared emotional experience. In emotionally starved couples it may be all the intimacy they've got. Thus, it may be repeatedly sought out because it is rewarding, being the only available source of closeness. Besides, after the blow-up he may be affectionate and sweet for a while, feeling guilty and fearing to lose her. She may back off a bit, partly to be safe, but partly because she's obtained the intimacy she needs, even though it be in this sad, sick, destructive form. The pressure's off for a while, and they settle down until she starts feeling lonely and comes looking for him again, only to start the next cycle.

Oddly enough, in other couples a fear of confrontation and anger can lead to an avoidance of intimacy. There are some people who thrive on conflict and confrontation. For example, patients with Borderline Personality Disorder have admitted to me that they will pick a fight with their mate when they get bored. Most of us, however, are troubled by conflict and seek to avoid it. The problem is, in any relationship, sooner or later there's going to be conflict. Say we have lunch together and both order key lime pie for dessert. The waiter comes back to report there's only one slice left. We've got conflict. In this case the conflict is pretty trivial and easy to resolve, since I also like the chess pie, pecan pie, chocolate pie, etc. But it may be a lot more serious in a marital conflict. In a long-term relationship the only way to avoid all conflict is to avoid dealing with any emotional issues, not to discuss problems, not to confront your spouse about anything. That is, **you can only avoid conflict by avoiding all intimacy in the relationship.** Couples who adopt this strategy simply drift apart and eventually lose track of each other altogether.

The solution to the intimacy problem follows the same conflict-resolution format outlined above. If the more intimate of the couple will quit pursuing so avidly and aggressively and back off a bit, the more distant spouse will feel more comfortable again. Eventually, he'll actually be desirous of more contact and may even seek out and approach his mate. If he can gradually learn to tolerate and even to enjoy more closeness and she can learn to tolerate a little more distance (without feeling rejected) they may become more alike in their desires for intimacy and achieve a mutually acceptable level of intimacy. The key here is to de-sensitize the distancer to his fear of intimacy by very gradual exposure to increasingly intimate relationships. He has to grow as a person, and that takes time and effort. The major pitfall is that she has to wait while her needs go largely unmet for a while. She has to grow too and perhaps develop other sources for intimacy or learn to entertain herself more. If she gets frustrated and grabs him, he'll run. Of course a related threat is that she'll find *all* her intimacy needs elsewhere by having an affair and ending the marriage. Some people in this situation get the idea they can have an affair to meet their intimacy needs and *not* end the marriage, and some of them are right. Some couples actually maintain and stabilize the marriage by keeping an affair going on the side, in a sense siphoning off some of the excess energy in the relationship. More commonly, the other spouse gets angry and leaves.

Part of the problem of arriving at mutually acceptable levels of intimacy is that the process of negotiating them is often done at a nonverbal level. If you feel close and loving towards your mate you move toward him or her physically, talk in a gentle tone of voice, and do things your mate finds considerate or thoughtful. If you're angry you clam up or slam the door, or stomp out of the house. *All* verbal communication is qualified by nonverbal messages. How you say something, when you say something, even choosing *not* to say something alters your verbal message. Your behavior talks. Thus, anything you do has communication value, at least potentially. In fact, your actions or nonverbal communication speaks "louder than words" because it has a stronger emotional response than does verbal communication. It is at the nonverbal level that we express emotion and it is at this level that we define our relationships. Your behavior tells me how you feel about me. In the absence of words, your nonverbal communication may be the only clue I've got as to the status of our relationship. Unfortunately, nonverbal communication is notoriously imprecise and subject to misinterpretation and misunderstanding. I am immediately moved emotionally if I happen upon you when you are crying, but I can't tell at first if you are heartbroken or deliriously happy. If you leave the room I'm in, it means something about our relationship, but the meaning is unclear. Are you angrily abandoning and rejecting me, or do you simply need some time alone? Does leaving mean you are comfortable with me but have an uncomfortably distended bladder?

In couples who don't communicate well verbally, each has only the other's behavior to go on, compounding the communication problem. Each will try to read the other's mind and feelings via their behavior alone, and they will frequently misinterpret or over-interpret each other. Thus, they end up reacting to a message the other hasn't actually intended to send, dealing with problems that aren't there, or that aren't what they seem to be. The solution to this problem, sensibly enough, is for the couple to communicate verbally, in words, not deeds, how they feel. They must tell each other openly how they feel about each other and their relationship. This includes verbally clarifying the meaning of their behavior, for example saying, "I'm not mad at you, just going outside to sit and think a while." Or saying, "Whenever I read a book at the dinner table it means I'm angry and don't want to talk to you."

Over time most couples get a lot better at reading each other's moods and feelings from their nonverbal communication. Couples who've been married for years may seem capable of reading each other's minds through some sort of psychic telepathy. However, even in these couples misunderstandings arise and require clarification from time to time. And some people never get very comfortable with talking about their relationship or expressing their feelings openly. As Paul Simon sang: "Some people never say those words 'I love you.' It's not their style to be so bold." In most couples there is a difference in how they wish to express their love for each other. In a sense, each of us has a certain unique "language of love," a way we want to express love and a way we want to *be* loved in return. If these couples are going to be happy, it is very helpful for each partner to learn to say, "I love you" in the language the other wants to hear, and equally important to learn to *feel* loved when the other partner expresses love in her own language. People who tend to prefer a good deal of distance in their marriage may still be expressing a lot of affection in their actions, perhaps completely unbeknownst to their mate. It may help the pursuer half of the couple to relax and feel more loved to learn how to interpret and appreciate these nonverbal messages. Even the simple act of coming home in the evening instead of hanging out at the local pub, says "I love you and want to be with you."

Closeness or intimacy demands honesty. You can't risk getting close to someone you don't trust, and you can't trust somebody who lies to you. It is useful, however, to distinguish between honesty and openness. Honesty means telling the truth. It means not lying, even in sophisticated, sneaky, indirect ways that aren't *actually* untrue but yet seek to deceive. Openness means revealing yourself, volunteering information about who you are and how you feel. **Honesty is an absolute requirement for marriage. You should *never* lie to your spouse. Openness, on the other hand, is negotiable.** How open you must be depends on how much intimacy you want. We'll look at this again in connection with the problem of infidelity, where the rules change and total openness is demanded. My usual rule for couples, however, is that they must be honest about everything, but need be open only about anything which potentially impacts the marriage. Something that happened years before you met is unlikely to affect the marriage, but if it does, it must be told. Other things may be at your own discretion. You don't need to report to your mate every time you see an attractive member of the opposite sex, even if there's a bit of nonsexual, friendly flirtation. If you're obsessed with the mail carrier, however, you need to tell. If you're in doubt about whether or not something needs telling, ask your spouse about it. If you're afraid to ask, it *definitely* needs telling. Meanwhile, don't forget that not being open means sacrificing some of the intimacy you got married for.

The Marital Needs of Men versus Women:
Another useful way of looking at marital differences is offered by Dr. Willard Harley, in his book *His Needs, Her Needs* (which we cited above.) Dr. Harley provides a list of the ten things people most need from their marital relationships. In alphabetical order they are:

Admiration
Affection
An attractive spouse
Conversation
Domestic support (i.e. housework)
Family commitment
Financial support
Honesty and openness
Recreational companionship (somebody to play with)
Sexual fulfillment.

Then Dr. Harley breaks the list down, according to sexes, listing the top five, in order of priority, for men versus women:

His Needs	*Her Needs*
Sexual fulfillment	Affection
Recreational companionship	Conversation
An attractive spouse	Honesty and openness
Domestic Support	Financial support
Admiration	Family commitment

You'll notice immediately that there's no overlap between these two lists. Both men and women need all these ten things from their marriages, but the top five for men are the bottom five for women, and vice versa. This leaves plenty of room for misunderstandings and conflict to develop, even if both are trying to help the other meet his or her needs. It is easy to assume that your mate needs what you do and end up failing to address her real needs and desires. You can be working hard and still have a frustrated, unfulfilled spouse.

Notice also that there's a certain complementarity to some of these needs. For example, he wants sex, while she wants affection. Affectionate sex constitutes "making love," as opposed to simply having intercourse. Sex and affection go hand-in-hand (as it were) if the couple recognize each other's different needs and try to oblige them. Or they can end up in a conflict with a self-perpetuating quality to it. When men aren't sexually fulfilled they tend to get mean, grouchy and unaffectionate. What woman wants to make love to such a man? So, she denies him sex, and he gets meaner, making it even less likely that she'll let him touch her. It's a vicious circle. Contrariwise, if he'll be sweet and affectionate with her, most women will become more desirous of sex. Being sexually satisfied, he'll continue to be affectionate, setting up a positive, self-sustaining cycle. This vicious cycle of no sex and no affection is frequently encountered in marriage counseling, and it can be a tough one to break. Unfairly, it is usually up to the wife to make the first move. It is simply easier to get her to agree to have sex than it is to get her husband to be nice without it.

Similarly, "he" wants someone to play with (recreational companionship) while "she" wants someone to talk to. Again there is a basis here for a mutually satisfying agreement. "If you'll go fishing with me, we can talk all you like." Or, he can sit like a statue all day, in which case she'll skip the next outing. Again, mutual understanding and cooperation allow a couple to meet both of their needs. Each is happy, getting their own needs met and each feels good about the other, as well as themselves.

Incidentally, I think Harley's list is a good one, but it's not universally valid. One could quibble about the order, for example. In particular, Admiration could probably be moved up to second or third place on most men's lists, as the male ego needs a lot of stroking. Further, I've seen couples who pretty nearly reversed roles and needs entirely, for example, with the wife much more sexually desirous and aggressive than the husband. So don't worry if you don't fit the profile exactly. Just remember to find out what your spouse truly needs and work together to see they are met, just as yours are.

John Gray (*Men Are from Mars; Women Are from Venus.*) also describes some dysfunctional relationship patterns that stem directly from gender-based differences. He notes, for example, that women generally prefer to talk out their problems with someone else, while men tend to go off alone to think them out for themselves. Men tend to become quickly bored or frustrated with the process of such a discussion and want to jump down to the bottom-line solution instead of slogging through the details. They want to take over the problem and fix it and may feel rejected, insulted, or inadequate if they aren't allowed to do so. Women, on the other hand, may be less outcome-oriented and find the discussion process to be helpful in itself. They may resent their husband's impatience and feel he hasn't really listened or understood. His "Mr. Fix-It" attitude may seem controlling or intrusive or disrespectful. Contrariwise, wives may feel rejected and excluded by their husbands' withdrawal to think things out alone, believing that if he loved and respected her he'd want to consult her about his problem. Meanwhile, the husband interprets her efforts to help as an indication she thinks he is incompetent to deal with his own problems.

As with the other male/female problems we've examined, the resolution to these is to recognize and accept that they simply represent different but equally valid ways of thinking and dealing with problems. Men can learn to shut up and listen attentively, especially if women can learn to tell the story more quickly or at least give some hint as to where it's going. Instead of feeling inadequate to solve his wife's problem, a man can feel like and truly be a helpful, competent listener– which is what she really needs. Instead of feeling rejected or put down, a woman can learn to respect her husband's privacy, admire his rugged individualism, and enjoy his company later, when he's feeling successful and happy.

Communication Skills:

So far we've looked at the differences that both attract couples together and pull them apart. We've talked about resolving these differences on a fairly abstract and global level. Now it's time to dig more specifically, into the nuts and bolts of conflict resolution, which is to say, of good marital communications. Couples often tell me they don't communicate. Technically, this cannot be true, since their behavior communicates something constantly. Even the behavior of not talking to each other definitely says something about the quality of their relationship. What they mean is that they don't communicate effectively. So we end up essentially learning good basic communication skills. Whole books have been written on these skills, but here's the crash course I give my patients:

Rules for Marital Problem-Solving:

1. No physical violence. This is an absolute rule and includes grabbing, pushing, hair-pulling, hitting or any other form of physical aggression. You can't have a marriage without trust and you can't trust somebody who hits you. Physical violence also gives an unfair advantage to the husband. Besides, it's illegal.

2. No alcohol during serious discussions. This doesn't mean you can't have a glass of wine with dinner or chat with your spouse over a beer or two. It does mean that you don't drink and fight. Alcohol tends to make you too emotional, irrational and impulsive to solve problems fairly and respectfully. Besides, even if you managed to arrive at an agreement, you probably wouldn't remember it in the morning.

3. No leaving or threatening to divorce in the course of an argument. This imminent threat to the very existence of the marriage renders the solving of specific problems impossible. How can we decide who has to wash the dishes when you're threatening to terminate the whole relationship? It also raises anxiety to panic levels. If you must talk about divorce, do it later, in a quiet, rational way. Threatening divorce in the middle of an argument is an unfair power tactic. If I make such a threat, you'll be so scared you'll give in, and I won't have to do the dishes.

4. No name-calling, cursing, threats or even vulgar language are permitted. These forms of communication constitute verbal violence, are disrespectful, and generate dysfunctional high levels of emotion. This kind of language does not facilitate but rather interferes with good communication. It is not the case that your mate will understand you better if you yell louder, and it isn't easy to kiss and make up with somebody who just called you a son of a bitch.

5. Be assertive, not aggressive (or passive-aggressive.) A marital argument is not like a debate or courtroom battle, but is rather an attempt to achieve mutual understanding. Therefore, express your viewpoint respectfully and without attacking your mate. Attacks lead only to counter-attacks, not to problem-solving.

6. Listen with an open mind to your spouse's view, and try to understand and respect it, not to change it. Again, your goal is to come to a mutual understanding, not to defeat your mate. If you did manage to defeat your spouse, you would then find yourself married to a loser, and very probably a sore loser, at that. What you want to achieve is a win-win resolution of the dispute.

7. Talk about the issues, not your spouse's character or personality flaws. Character assassination is disrespectful and unloving, and it defines the problem in unsolvable terms. You can't very readily change your personality, but you can change your behavior. The issue isn't whether or not you are "lazy", but rather your failure to do your chores as agreed. I can't change the fact that I am "slovenly" by nature, but if I start picking up my stuff you won't care about that little flaw in my character.

8. Don't interrupt. This is distracting and disrespectful and another unfair power tactic.

9. Stick to one topic at a time. "Shot-gunning" is another power tactic and prevents focusing on any one issue. Thus, no issue gets resolved. If there are several issues to deal with, make an agenda and go

item by item, just as in any business meeting.

10. No monologues, speeches, or diatribes allowed. Dominating the conversation is another unfair power tactic that impedes the process of coming to a mutual understanding.

11. No mind-reading or psychoanalyzing. Respond to what your partner says, not to what you assume he "really" means. Mind-reading is manipulative and places the other at a disadvantage, facing the impossible task of defending his unconscious mind.

12. Don't play the "blame game." Assigning blame doesn't solve the problem, and in a relationship both sides usually have some share of the blame. This is because of the circular nature of relationships. Whatever you do is both a reaction to and a cause of your spouse's behavior, and vice versa. "I drink because you nag," but then you nag because I drink! Thus, you can go back and forth ad infinitum, assigning the blame without ever coming to an agreement. Instead, fix the problem.

13. Avoid drawing third parties into the discussion. This distracts you from the real problem, which is the marital relationship itself. People do this– e.g. talk about someone's mother– because it takes the heat off the couple and diverts it to someone else. But this renders the problem unsolvable, because you can't change the third party.

14. Don't bring up the past. It's not possible to follow this one absolutely, since the past is father to the present and therefore relevant to the current discussion. But rehashing the unchangeable past

prevents present and future change. Besides, it's not fair, or useful, to keep punishing somebody for the same old crimes. Learn from the past and move on.

15. Agree to disagree but to cooperate anyway. It isn't necessary for the two of you to agree in principle, only in practice. Arguments rarely change anyone's mind in truly fundamental ways. Your spouse will never convince you that football is the ultimate form of entertainment, so why do you think you can sell him that Brussels sprouts taste good? Fortunately, agreement in theory isn't required. What is required is that you agree to act in unison or coordination. I may think your way of saving money is nuts, and you think mine is idiotic, but if I agree to do it your way anyhow, we've got a deal that will work.

16. Keep your word, and follow through on all agreements, even if you change your mind. It's a trust issue: no agreement is worth a thing if it isn't carried out faithfully, and if you renege this time, I'm not much interested in negotiating with you next time. Get back to your mate and renegotiate a new deal, but don't rewrite one unilaterally.

17. Compromise. This is the real key to solving marital problems and resolving disputes. Both sides give a little and both get a little. Both feel their views and needs have been respected, and both act in a loving manner to their spouse. This is a win-win solution, the goal of all marital discussions. But it will only happen if you approach the discussion in an open-minded and respectful way and demonstrate a

willingness to sacrifice for the good of your family. 18. Use **The Rule** to end over-heated arguments. The Rule (which I did not originate, but which I often recommend) **specifies that either spouse can call a halt to the discussion at any time and the argument *must* end immediately.** However, in so doing, that spouse promises to resume the discussion at an agreed upon time, say in one hour. The reason for this is that in many marriages one spouse is threatened by conflict and confrontation, feels trapped, and must escape. This threatens the other, who feels abandoned and rejected and is compelled to pursue the discussion to a resolution. (Recall that people experience panic attacks when they feel either trapped or abandoned; this marital situation has the potential to produce both these emotions, and thus a whole lot of panic and uproar.) The Rule meets the needs of both spouses, to a degree, by temporarily ending the conflict, but guaranteeing it will be resumed in a brief time. If both follow it absolutely, it will work.

These rules are only a thumbnail sketch of good communication skills, and many more could be added. Following them, however, should greatly enhance your marital communications and increase the probability of working out your conflicts. What these rules do is to mandate mutually respectful communication. **Key concepts are to be assertive, not aggressive; try to understand your spouse's position; and negotiate to a mutually acceptable compromise.** This is a lot harder than it sounds, but the effort is well worth it in the long run. Without these communication and conflict resolution skills, there may *be* no long run.

Chapter Nine. In the Long Run
In The Long Run:

Happy marriages tend to last a lifetime, but that doesn't mean they are without conflicts, crises, and concerns. People and circumstances change, and marital relationships must change accordingly, or the marriage may fail. Indeed, it is at transition points, times of rapid change, that marriages tend to fall apart. Some of these are "bolts from the blue" and can't be predicted or prevented. One spouse has a psychotic break and the other finds she can't live with a fellow who thinks he's Moses and doesn't choose to bathe. Some derive from fundamental differences that never mattered before, but do so now, and can't be resolved. For example, a Jew and a Catholic may do fine until children come along. He goes to temple, she to Mass, and perhaps they ecumenically attend some of each other's services. But when Junior is born there are serious choices to make: a baptism or a Bris, for example. Now the religious difference comes to matter a great deal. And this is a difference people find hard to compromise on. It's also one that should have been anticipated and dealt with in premarital counseling. But then, young people in love tend to overlook problems and believe everything is possible and no problem is too big for them. (Despite this difficulty, I believe premarital counseling is extremely helpful and should be obtained by all couples entering matrimony. I am frequently amazed to see couples who've been married for years yet have no idea of each other's basic values, beliefs, goals, or life-plans, having never even discussed them.)

Stages and Transitions:

Other changes and transition points in marriages are normal, predictable parts of the developmental sequence all marriages go through. These can be anticipated and prevented, or at least mitigated. This too is the subject of whole books, but it warrants a brief sketch here. (For one way of looking at the marital life cycle, see *In Search of the Mythical Mate*, by Bade and Pearson.) Actually, we've already alluded to some of these developmental changes, in looking at the in-love phenomenon.

Just as human infants go through a normal, predictable growth process, maturing through identifiable developmental stages, so also does marriage have a developmental cycle or sequence. Indeed, the whole family, with the marriage at its core, goes through a sequence of developmental stages. Making the transition from one stage to the next is difficult, requiring growth both in the individuals and in their ways of relating to one another. This phase shift can result in a marital crisis, or, for that matter, in an individual depression, existential crisis, extramarital affair, illness, or many other problems. They are easier to negotiate, however, if they are understood and recognized to be normal developmental challenges.

The first developmental challenge to a marriage is for the two individuals to learn how

to see themselves as and to act like a "couple."
Marriage is very much a team sport; you either win
as a team or lose as a team. You can't have a
marriage in which one spouse always wins and the
other loses. Marriage begins with two individual
players learning to be team players, to act in a
coordinated fashion, to see themselves as belonging
to an organic entity larger than themselves. An
individual goes to the hoop, seeking the glory of
being high-point man. A team player sacrifices his
own stats for the good of the team and passes off to a
teammate who has a clearer shot. On a team, the
high scorer hangs his head in shame with the rest
when they lose a game. After all, his hot-dogging
may have contributed to the team's loss. On a
winning team, even the subs get to drink champagne
with the starters; it's a *team* victory.

Learning to be part of a couple isn't always easy,
especially for men. Men are by nature and nurture
independent and self-directing, prone to look out for
themselves and used to living alone. Suddenly they
find themselves having to account for their time,
check-in constantly before making plans, share their
hard-earned money, and give up carousing with their
buddies. For many men this threatens their
masculinity and makes them feel like little boys,
dominated by their mothers. They feel emasculated
and controlled and respond by rebelling against their
wife/mother and acting-out irresponsibly. The wife
feels rejected and insecure and may respond by
acting like a disciplinary mother to his rebellious

child. Suddenly, we have a full-blown, negative transference (as opposed to the positive transference of being in-love) in which a couple are acting like an angry mother and a rebellious child instead of two mature adults. Conflict and chaos are the results. Some couples resolve the problem by allowing the husband to "act single," chasing girls and drinking beer, while the wife essentially goes home to her mother. This team simply fails to gel at all and divorce or annulment soon follows.

Fortunately, for most couples, the honeymoon glow of being in love and the courtship process itself lead to a bonding together and the formation of a true marriage. "Wedded" truly means welded together, bonded or glued into one unit. Two individuals come together to forge a kind of symbiotic union, an organic entity, that in some ways recreates the symbiosis that exists between a mother and her baby. This is a powerful emotional experience that should lead to an indissoluble, lifetime union. It's been called "the illusion of fusion."

It really is, of course, to some extent an illusion. Yes, the two are bonded and form a couple, a living being larger than themselves. And it is essential that they see themselves this way and commit themselves to sacrifice for the good of that union. But they are still individuals as well. At some point they must progress to the next developmental challenge, the challenge of staying together as a couple while resuming their lives as individual persons. Here timing is often a problem, as one member of the pair may be ready to move on while the other wants to hang on to the honeymoon a while longer. Like a toddler ready to separate from his mom and head out into the world, one spouse tries to pursue his or her own private interests (which may be career, hobby, friendship, or other interests), forgoing the constant togetherness of the couple stage. This threatens the other who perceives it as a rejection and feels abandoned and betrayed. This spouse tries to hang on to the other, who then feels trapped and controlled. A crisis of intimacy and power occurs, with all the powerful emotions generated by feeling trapped or abandoned. The couple finds itself in the distance/pursuer conflict described above. As before, the solution is understanding, acceptance, and compromise. The distance needs to proceed more slowly towards increased independence, reassure his spouse that he isn't leaving her, and spend more time alone with his wife. The pursuer needs to let go, try to share in her husband's growth, and find new avenues to explore on her own.

About the time most couples get these basic "couple" issues worked out and find themselves comfortable in their marriage, along comes the next developmental challenge: trying to make *three* someones happy. There isn't much comfortable or convenient about having babies. They change everything in your life. They cry, they get sick, they produce gross bodily products. They don't sleep right, and neither do you. My brother likens them to black holes in space, sucking up all the energy around them. This can put an enormous strain on a marital relationship. The couple must learn to function together as parents. They must each develop a relationship with the infant as well as learning how to relate differently to each other. Relationships with their newly grand-parented moms and dads may also change dramatically, and control issues may arise along with jealousies and ownership disputes. Many new mothers become so enmeshed with their children that they effectively reject and neglect their husbands. Many husbands are intimidated by the sudden responsibility of supporting a family; others are jealous of the baby who's taken over first place in their wife's affections. Power struggles may erupt around issues of discipline, new baby chores, in-laws. Most couples will meet the challenge of parenthood and become better people for it, as well as more closely wedded. Others won't survive. Over the years I've seen a lot of young mothers having to go it alone because their husbands bailed out when the wives became pregnant or stayed barely long enough to give the kid a name. The critical issues are whether the couple can learn to make personal sacrifices for the good of the family and whether they can keep the marriage vital and gratifying while putting their relationship temporarily in the background. Team play is essential, another reason I encourage fathers to take a very active role in caring for their babies.

Other developmental challenges will come, some big, some small, as a couple's life together

unfolds. With the birth of a second child, sibling issues must be dealt with. How do you divide your time; who's your favorite; what is fair treatment of both kids; how do you handle conflicts and jealousies between the children? Then comes the "school daze" stage of family life, in which everyone in the family must learn to interface differently with the outside world. Then there's Little League, with issues about competence and competition. This is soon followed by the entry of the first child into puberty and adolescence, with its identity crises, rebelliousness, mood swings and hormonal acting-out. Adolescence leads to the Leaving Home stage of the family life cycle, in which children grow up and move out on their own– hopefully. This stage represents a radical transformation of the family and the marriage and is uniquely challenging, as we briefly noted above.

To this point in its life a family has been growing, first with two individuals becoming a couple, than with the addition of children. Now the family begins to shrink, as its progeny are launched into the world to establish their own families. Ultimately all the children will be gone, leaving only the original pair to deal with the "empty nest" stage of married life. Many families have great difficulty with this stage, and some never manage to handle this transition. Marital issues which have long been submerged begin to reappear as they can no longer be detoured into child-rearing issues. Couples who have lost track of themselves as husband and wife, who have related only as parents, find the prospect of being alone together quite daunting. They may have little left in common except the children, and the grandkids aren't yet in sight. Since the children are all that's holding the marriage together, their departure can mean the failure and dissolution of the marriage. And in fact, this period shows up as a peak on the charts of when marriages end in divorce. Many couples solve the problem by hanging on to a problem child, who, for some reason, fails to grow up and leave home. They continue to function as parents for this problem child and thus they remain together. Unfortunately, this entails the sacrifice of this child, who can never grow up, but must stay impaired, and at home, to keep his parents together.

This scenario lies behind many young adult failures. The young person may drop out of school, repeatedly get fired, go crazy, do drugs or bounce in and out of grossly inappropriate marriages. Anything that forces him to stay home and be parented will suffice. The treatment for such couples, as described by family therapist Jay Haley (*Leaving Home*) is for the parents to work together and insist on mature, responsible behavior in the "child." This may even involve tossing the miscreant out of the house to support himself. Then they work on the marriage.

For many couples the empty nest stage of life is a happy one and a time for great intimacy in the marriage. Becoming grandparents is usually not much of a crisis, though it does necessitate learning to relate differently to your children (respecting their authority as the parents of your grandchildren). Later life offers more developmental challenges, first dealing with your aged and dying parents, then with your own aging and the death of a spouse. By this time most of the weak marriages have already fallen apart, but it isn't so rare to see forty or fifty year marriages succumb to the temptation of a late-life fling or break up in a battle for custody of grandchildren as their own parents divorce. And many other marriages persist, but have little or nothing in the way of real intimacy or love, sustained by fear of being old and alone or perhaps by sheer momentum.

Commitment:

What determines which marriages will survive and which will fail in the long run? **More than anything else it is the degree of commitment the partners have to each other and to the marriage.** Falling in love is an act of emotion. **Mature marital love, on the other hand, is primarily an act of will.** As one of my patients pointed out to me, the preacher doesn't ask you how you *feel*, but rather what you will *do*. "Will you take this man/woman to be your lawful wedded husband/wife?" Your answer is "I *will*." "Do you promise to love, honor, etc.?" You reply, "I *do*." Marriage succeeds when both spouses are truly committed to each other, to their marriage as something larger than themselves, and to doing the work it will take to make the marriage work out. Learning to understand and accept each other is hard work. Learning to communicate effectively and resolve conflicts is hard work. Growing, changing yourself and your ways of relating, dealing with changes in your partner, takes real effort. You won't do this kind of work unless you're really committed.

Unfortunately, many people now enter into marriage without this level of commitment. Their attitude is essentially "I'll stay as long as it's good, but if it gets too tough, I'll just split." All marriages have tough times, so if this is the attitude, divorce becomes almost a certainty, right from the start. In the old days divorce was extremely difficult to obtain, both legally and societally. Our society strongly supported the institution of marriage and just as strongly frowned on divorce. Now, there's little stigma attached to divorce, and our social institutions no longer provide a support system for marriage. At the same time that we demand more and more from our marriages, we make it harder for them to persist and make divorce easy to obtain. Marriage in our society today is expected to provide all our needs for intimacy, sexuality, companionship, parenting, and financial support. It is no longer just for procreation, child-rearing and financial purposes. Yet, there is precious little societal support for marriage and almost no training provided in how to make marriage work. Even the churches have mostly acquiesced to divorce as the norm and most provide more support for the newly divorced than the newly married.

With little social support, what's left to keep marriages together? Commitment. In sickness and in health, for richer or poorer, in good times and bad, marriages survive because the couple are truly committed to each other and to their marriage. Divorce is unthinkable to a truly committed couple. It would seem like cutting yourself off from your family. Indeed, it *is* cutting yourself off from the family you've created together. A real, genuine, deep and unquestioning commitment to each other provides the foundation on which a family is built and the basis for solving whatever problems arise. If you're truly committed, you *must* solve your problems, because you're stuck with each other, and you *can* solve them because you can trust the other to stay with you and work things out.

A few years into our marriage my wife and I had a serious, even heated discussion while on vacation. It was about one of the biggies like money or sex. We spoke our minds, respectfully (I hope) but frankly. When we concluded that we had no more to say and couldn't resolve the argument that evening, we agreed to table it and went out for a pleasant meal together. Later I marveled at our ability to do this and puzzled over how we'd done it. Then I realized we had another fifty years to work this thing out, so there was really no particular urgency and no reason to spoil a good evening. We were committed to each other and our marriage and to resolving our differences in a mutually satisfactory manner. With a half century to work it out, the pressure was off for that evening– and in the long run we *had* to work it out or drive each other crazy. **Commitment makes marriage work.**

When I work with a couple in therapy, I see many factors contributing to the success or failure of their marriage. Have they chosen wisely, selecting a person they can learn to love and live with? Do they have a good support system in extended family, friends, church? Do they have good models in their families of origin? Do they have good basic communication skills? Are they willing to look honestly at themselves, admit to their failings and change themselves? Are they really trying to understand, accept, value, and emulate each other? What external factors or events are helping or hindering? (Luck helps, for example in not getting transferred to Maine when your spouse takes a job in Arizona.) But most of all I try to assess their level of commitment to each other. Truly committed couples *feel* different to me. They are truly wedded together, part of an organic entity with a life of its own. Divorce is unthinkable in the same way an amputation would be. They belong to each other, and at some level they know it. These couples will succeed in making a happy marriage because they are committed to doing so. They will do well in therapy, because they are committed to the process of reconciliation and rebuilding that is therapy.

Finally, **it is my observation that happy people make happy marriages.** Many people marry because they are unhappy and they expect their partner and the marriage to solve this problem. In effect, their wedding gift to their new spouse is their own unhappiness and their demand for the spouse to make them happy. It's a pretty poor present. Unhappy people marry and make each other miserable. **Learn to be happy first, on your own, then find another happy person and share your happiness with each other.** I've seen many people search desperately for years to find a mate who will make them happy. They end up in all sorts of bizarre and destructive relationships built around dependency needs, depression, insecurity, and fantasy. They try to make obviously non-viable relationships work out and hang on much too long when relationships fail. Oddly enough, if they finally quit looking for someone to make them happy and set about doing this for themselves instead, a strange thing happens. They find someone they can be happy with. This is because happy people are magnetic; they draw people to them without even trying. Make yourself happy and a relationship will probably find you. Further, by making yourself happy you'll have reprogrammed your unconscious and will find yourself attracted to people who are much more appropriate as potential mates. If you don't find someone, that's okay too, because you're already making yourself happy on your own.

Chapter Ten. Infidelity
Infidelity:

When I was in graduate school (early '70's) the "open marriage" was very much in fashion. This charming theory held that for truly loving couples monogamy and sexual fidelity were unnecessary and overly confining. Marriages should be opened to include other sexual partners, with the full knowledge and consent of the spouses. Having sex with others would enhance your life personally and even enhance your marriage as you "shared your love" with other people. In those days many of my fellow grad students were involved in such open marriages, freely and openly having affairs whenever the opportunity arose. It wasn't uncommon for both spouses and both paramours to share a house together. These couples assured everyone that they were quite comfortable with their open marriages and indeed they all seemed very relaxed, gracious, accepting and loving about it all. A lot of pot smoking probably helped as well. This was a truly loving, generous, intelligent and enlightened group of people in many ways. Yet, every one of these open marriages fell apart and ended in divorce. Why?

In the long run, affairs simply don't work. We just aren't programmed, whether biologically or culturally, to accept infidelity on the part of our mates. Actually, evolutionary biologists will argue that men and women may be programmed differently in this regard, at a biological level. These theorists assume that a primary motivation for all higher animals is to pass on their genetic material. Behavior which accomplishes this is perpetuated because more offspring survive to reproduce themselves, carrying the genes for these behavior traits. Starting from these basic assumptions, the theory holds that a male's best reproductive strategy is to impregnate as many females as possible and then move on. This strategy produces a lot of progeny and leaves their care and feeding to others. Hopefully, one of the many offspring will survive to procreate, while the male saves his energy for more reproducing, not child-rearing. Females, on the other hand, *must* stay home and nurse their babies. Their best bet is to raise a smaller number of children to adulthood, with the help of a loyal, long-term mate. Or, in words variously attributed to Dorothy Parker and every other quotable person since Socrates: "Hogamus, higamus, men are polygamous; Higamus, hogamus, women monogamous." This may be true, biologically, and it seems to work fine in many cultures. Arab emeers have their harems and the Frenchman has his mistress, and nobody seems to squawk much. But psychologically this will not work today in our society. Whatever his biological programming, today's American male will not stay married long if he continues to stray.

In an egalitarian marriage, having affairs is "cheating." It is the taking of something you are not entitled to and have vowed to forswear. It is a violation of a sacred covenant. (In Christian tradition marriage is a holy sacrament, a contract made in the eyes of God.) At the very heart of a loving relationship it places a lie, a betrayal of the most basic trust. It is impossible to have an affair without deceit. The affair makes your vow of fidelity a lie, not to mention the lies you must tell about late-night "work sessions," unexplainable restaurant bills, and who's making the hang-up phone calls. The marriage fails because you can't live with somebody you don't trust, and you can't trust somebody who lies to you. This is especially true as regards the most intimate bond in the marital relationship, namely sex.

Rebuilding Trust:

In working with couples who have experienced an affair, family therapists find that rebuilding shattered trust is the crucial task. As my friend and teacher Frank Pittman points out in his excellent study of affairs, *Private Lies*, spouses aren't happy about the sexual transgression, but they can usually get past it. What they can't forgive is the lie. Unless they can re-establish honesty and trust, these couples will end up in court. For trust to exist, two things are required:

1. Both parties must be trustworthy, i.e. honest, and
2. Both must *decide* to trust the other.

Asking your mate to trust you when you are still lying to her is asking her to be a fool. This is not a nice thing to do to the love of your life. Thus, *complete* honesty is required. Ordinarily, I advise that in a marriage you must be absolutely honest about everything; however, you do not necessarily need to be completely *open*. That is, you must never lie, but you needn't "tell all" about irrelevant items (unless you've agreed to.) You don't have to reveal secrets about your past life, private fantasies, hidden vices, etc., unless they potentially impact the marriage. Your spouse may not need to know about a fling you had at eighteen, years before you met–unless there's a chance an illegitimate child is going to show up some day looking for college money or you've got a transmittable disease. Some couples agree to be totally open as well as honest, and that's okay, too (though the gain in intimacy may be offset by having to deal with painful things you didn't really need to know about in the first place.) When there's been an affair, however, complete openness as well as honesty must be the rule. Your loyalty must be to the marriage, not the affair, so *all* must be revealed. Following Dr. Pittman's advice, I instruct my couples that for six months (Pittman gives them two years, but I find this too long for most to handle) the injured party can ask *anything* about the affair, and the adulterer must answer fully and honestly. After six months they are to shut up and never bring it up again. I also caution the faithful partner to think carefully before asking, because once they know the awful details, they'll never forget them. This rule provides the honesty essential to rebuilding trust, but also puts a statute of limitations on the obsessive interrogations about the affair.

It is logically impossible to prove a negative proposition, for example that flying dragons do not exist. Granted, nobody has seen any, much less caught one on film, but that could be because dragons are really sneaky and move too fast to be seen by human eyes. You can't disprove the existence of aliens, Bigfoot, ESP, leprechauns or anything else. No matter how much evidence you assemble, you also can't prove you're not having an affair. There's no way you can have proof positive that something is *not happening.* A woman I was seeing told me she was absolutely positive her husband wasn't cheating on her. They went to bed together, woke up together, drove together to the store where both worked, and drove home together for the evening. Neither went out to clubs, hobbies, etc. without the other. So she knew his whereabouts twenty-four hours a day. But the husband later revealed to me that his wife was a very sound sleeper. After she drifted off to dreamland he drifted off to see his mistress.

Because there can be no absolute proof that the adulterer is now faithful, the second requirement for re-establishing trust after an affair is to take a leap of faith. You must *decide* to trust the unfaithful spouse, knowing you've been deceived in the past and could be again. This is hard to do. Trusting again means you can be hurt again, made to look foolish, kicked again while you're still down. But it is essential if the marriage is to be preserved. How can anyone reasonably choose to believe a spouse who has manifestly lied?

Figure it this way: If you foolishly decide not to trust a spouse who would in fact have been faithful and true, you've saved your pride, but lost a good marriage and been unfair to your reformed mate. If you lovingly decide to trust and your spouse cheats again, at least you know you've done the right and loving thing, though you will pay for it by being terribly hurt. Either way you could end up looking like a fool, but you get to decide which is worse, to be a fool for pride or a fool for love. To "love not wisely but too well" seems the nobler, but also the harder choice. It also contradicts the popular saying "Fool me once; shame on you. Fool me twice; shame on me."

Yet, surprisingly, it's not uncommon for couples to stay together after an affair. Many actually grow closer together and are happier than ever. It requires an amazing capacity for forgiveness, but from couples I've seen, it's worth it. Divorce is a nightmare to be avoided if at all possible. Don't throw away a good marriage because somebody made a mistake. **Good people do bad things sometimes.**

People have affairs for all sorts of reasons, and in marriage counseling it is useful to examine why this particular affair occurred. Is it a one-time thing or a repeated pattern? Does it reflect a problem in the marriage or is it symptomatic of a personality disorder in one of the spouses? What people say about their motivation does not always accurately reflect the real situation. Perhaps surprisingly, many affairs are not primarily about sex and some aren't overtly sexual at all (especially nowadays when they may be conducted over the Internet.) Affairs are variously motivated, but most are basically about getting someone to pay attention to you and tell you how wonderful you are. Here's a thumbnail sketch of some of the reasons people have affairs and what implications they may have for marriages.

Why People Have Affairs:
Some affairs barely qualify as such and have little, if anything, to say about the marriages of those involved. A man at an out-of-town conference has a few drinks with fellow attendees at the hotel bar. As the evening wears on, they adjourn to his hotel room for a few more nightcaps. He awakes the next morning to find himself naked, sharing his bed with an equally nude woman. Both are ashamed of themselves, though neither has a clear memory of what, if anything, has occurred. They dress and leave without conversation and part company forever. One would have to label this an affair, despite its brevity and lack of emotional involvement. However, it's not much of an affair and it says nothing fundamentally important about their marriages. It says their judgement is poor. These people don't have a marital problem (or at least they *didn't* have one). They have a drinking problem.

Dr. Pittman describes affairs that happen out of

politeness. A woman in distress turns for solace to a long-time male co-worker. He comforts her with a hug and the two confuse this sudden intimacy with sexuality. She kisses him passionately and he's too polite to say no to her advances. Again, this "affair" does not necessarily imply a marital problem, just a lack of sophistication and assertiveness skills. More pathologically, but still not reflecting a marital problem per se, there are "philanderers" who constantly, chronically, and compulsively seek out one extramarital partner after another. These are mostly men and often the sons of philandering fathers who taught them to behave this way. Some of these are so-called "sex addicts" who require constant sexual stimulation to sustain their endorphin levels and make themselves "happy." Most of them don't really like women very much and many don't even like sex anymore. What they like is *scoring*, and they are driven to score one after another, amassing huge numbers of conquests, if possible. Some of these pathetic men are sociopaths who like to use women; some are sadists who like to hurt women; some are power-trippers who want to dominate women, perhaps because they fear being dominated by women. All of them are seriously disturbed in some way, though many of them function quite nicely in other areas of life. Many philanderers are narcissistic personalities who feel compelled to obtain the worshipful attention of countless women. (Several U.S. Presidents come to mind.) In any case, philanderers have a personal problem as regards sex, gender, and honesty. Their wives find it hard to accept, but their husbands' behavior has nothing to do with them or the marital relationship. Philanderers do not carry on so because the wife is too old, unattractive or unloving, but because of their own personal compulsions. And the marriage may actually be pretty sound in many ways. In fact, the wife is often pretty happy until she discovers her husband's infidelity and begins rocking the boat.

If there's a "typical" affair, it is probably two friends or co-workers whose relationship gradually takes on a sexual dimension. It begins innocently enough and there is a genuine, reality-based affection and respect between them. But many of us are so tied to gender in our relationships that we find it difficult to be simply friends or associates with those of the opposite sex. Any close relationship must be sexually bonded. So at some point fantasy and flirtation become overt seduction and a choice is made, perhaps impulsively and often under the influence of alcohol. It may be a one-time-only kind of thing or may go on for twenty years. It may be primarily sexual or more of a friendship with very little actual sex, but there is always a strong emotional attachment as well.

This kind of affair may run its course and die out quietly, lead to an explosive confrontation, or produce a divorce and subsequent remarriage. There are many ways such an affair can end badly, and the prospects for long-term happy outcomes are pretty bleak. These affairs produce a lot of fights, a lot of divorces, broken friendships, employment terminations, and a few homicides and suicides. They can be quite explosive, even deadly. A few years ago, a woman and her boyfriend came to enlist my help with her alcoholic husband. She was leaving him to be with her paramour, but the husband had threatened to kill her and himself if she left. I made an appointment to see husband and wife the next day and advised her not to go home, but to lay low until then. She didn't go home, but she did go to her office, and he shot her dead in the parking deck. His body was found a couple of days later.

Most affairs don't end so violently, but they rarely work out happily for anybody involved. Sometimes one spouse gets divorced, then waits for years for the other to follow suit. These can produce tremendous heartache and, ultimately, bitterness, as the frustrated divorcee gradually realizes her lover is *never* going to leave his spouse. In such cases the spouse often knows of the affair and doesn't object to it, so long as the marriage remains intact. Then they threaten suicide, have a nervous breakdown, threaten to cause a public scandal, or whatever it takes to hang on to the adulterous partner. Even where the two lovers both divorce and then marry each other, research indicates, and my clinical experience confirms, such marriages usually fail. Mistrust and guilt and the animosity of exes, children, and family weigh down the new marriage beyond its capacity to bear. How can you ever trust someone when you know he cheated on his last wife-- with you? When you feel overwhelmed with guilt over the affair and broken marriage, how can you not be angry at the person who turned you into an adulterer? How can you not go crazy when your new spouse demands absolute perfection in her new family, to make up for abandoning the old one? The deck is very much stacked against marriages that begin as affairs, and I doubt that more than about twenty per cent succeed.

So what's the appeal of an affair? It's partly the excitement of discovering someone new, exploring sex with a new body. It's partly the thrill of being in love again and the ego boost of having someone in love with you. Further, sexual passion is enhanced by the cops-and-robbers secrecy and intrigue of an affair, not to mention the sweet delight of doing something naughty. More than anything else, an affair is about having someone devote his or her time exclusively to you, pay total attention to you, and tell you in every possible way how wonderful you are. Time together may be quite limited, but it is always a time of exclusive one-on-one attention, with no kids, dogs, spouses, yard work or telephones to interrupt you. It's a fantasy come true, a cheap and passionate, but ultimately superficial intimacy. There are no arguments over money, no household chores and no issues to resolve. What marriage can compete with that? (Which is why the affair must end and *all* contact cease before marriage counseling can be effective.)

What affairs don't offer, but what adulterers

usually say they are seeking, is true and lasting intimacy. Intimacy, by its nature, thrives on honest revelation of self. Affairs are based on deceit. They provide the illusory pseudo-intimacy of illicit passion. If you're truly seeking intimacy, you are much more likely to find it at home, in the security of a committed marital relationship. That, however, requires work and taking chances and looking honestly at yourself. Affairs are safer, in the sense that what you reveal to your lover will stay secret, just as the whole relationship is to be kept secret. But a lie is not a firm basis for any relationship.

This last kind of affair may have serious implication about the quality of the marital relationship. If there is not enough intimacy in a marriage, some spouses will look elsewhere for it, or at least be receptive when it offers itself to them. If the sexual relationship is unsatisfactory, people may look elsewhere to meet their needs. If one spouse is too controlling, the other may seek a haven where he is allowed to be himself. In highly conflictual marriages, a spouse may simply be looking for a quiet port sheltered from the storm, or perhaps an ally to take their side and tell them how cruelly their spouse mistreats them. In all these cases, the affair points accurately to a genuine problem in the marital relationship. Something is broken and needs to be fixed, even after the affair itself is over and has been dealt with.

In many cases the break isn't all that bad and can be readily mended. For example, I worked with a couple in which the wife had an affair of several years' duration with her husband's business partner. The husband was something of a workaholic, staying at the office until late each night. The partner, meanwhile, was taking care of his *home* "business." When discovered, the wife immediately gave up the affair entirely and begged for forgiveness. He loved her, so he swallowed his pride, took her back, and cut way back on his work hours to spend more time with her. Fifteen years later they are still together and happier than ever. The business partnership, on the other hand, was dissolved.

In counseling with couples who have experienced an extramarital affair we always ask what meaning the affair has about the state of the marital relationship. Is there a problem in the marriage which has, in some way, contributed to the likelihood of one spouse having an affair? However, we also make it clear that marital problems neither *caused* nor *justify* the affair. It is not okay to have an affair even if your wife nags you, your husband is obsessed with ESPN, or you and your mate can't resolve your money issues. Solve the problem. Nor can anyone *make* you have an affair, no matter how offensive or seductive their behavior. You are responsible for your own choices and conduct. I did, however, once see a surprisingly plain woman who'd been involved in dozens of affairs because her husband insisted on it. He got a perverse pleasure from hearing her descriptions of these tawdry encounters. She was sick of it and quit, knowing he'd probably divorce her, which he promptly did.

Jealousy:
    Closely related to the topic of infidelity is the issue of **jealousy.** Jealousy is a mixture of emotions including a fear of losing your love to another person, resentment of the presumed interloper, and mistrust or suspicion of your partner. It is an unpleasant emotion to experience either in yourself or in your mate, and it leads to unpleasant and destructive behavior. Jealous people falsely accuse others, possessively control their spouses, and generally conduct themselves in a petty and childish manner. More seriously, they've been known to shoot people in a fit of jealous rage.

    It is popularly believed that jealousy is an indicator of deep, true love. It is not. Well, maybe a brief moment of mild jealousy indicates love, but severe and sustained jealousy signals that something is seriously wrong. This kind of jealousy indicates not love but insecurity. The jealous person simply doesn't believe that he is lovable enough for anyone to be faithful to him. It isn't really the other that he doubts; it is himself. This is why denials of affairs and protestations of love have little impact on the jealous mate. He is not reassured because he still mistrusts himself.

    Jealous people try to control their mate's every move, in order to prevent them from contacting a potential new lover. They bug the phones, follow their partner's car, snoop around in their dresser drawers. They interrogate in ridiculous detail and over-interpret the answers in truly paranoid fashion. Needless to say, this kind of control and harassment is decidedly unpleasant to live with. Most people will either leave the relationship or decide to go ahead and take a lover, both as a pleasant relief and because they're already being punished for doing so.

Sometimes jealousy is an indication of a slightly different kind of insecurity. The jealous partner doesn't believe his mate could be faithful because he isn't faithful himself. Thus, I keep a high index of suspicion when a highly jealous, possessive, suspicious spouse comes into my office. It often turns out that the one doing all the questioning and accusing is also the one already having an affair. Meanwhile, the other spouse is generally confused and befuddled by this crazy and vicious game and may genuinely wonder about her own sanity.

How do you handle jealous feelings? First, you work on self-esteem and self-love issues. Take away the source of your jealous insecurity by learning to accept and value yourself as a person, so you can believe in someone else's love. Then you decide to trust your partner and avoid suspicious thoughts. My wife and I stumbled onto an interesting way to do this: in our wedding vows we promised not only to be faithful but also to trust in the other's fidelity as well. That means I violate my wedding vows just to *think* suspiciously or jealously. For some reason this helps. I'm not allowed to think jealous thoughts, so I don't.

Many men today find themselves married to women who work closely, on a daily basis, with men. The opportunity for an affair is always there, and they feel threatened. Some of them get jealous and try to keep the wife faithful by controlling her, keeping her narrowly confined or caged in. As we've seen, this is more likely to chase her away than keep her. Besides, who wants a spouse who stays with them and is faithful to them only because she *has to*? I figure it's better to give her total freedom. Then, if she comes back to you each night it's because she *wants* to. That makes you feel good. In fact, you can tell yourself you must be a heckuva guy to hang on to such a desirable and independent woman. "But my wife likes men and men like her," some men say. Of course. Do you really want to be married to a woman who doesn't like men? Or to one who isn't desirable to men?

Chapter Eleven. Other Issues in Marriage Finances:

Next to control over the TV remote, the biggest power struggle I see in marriages is usually over money. We've already looked at the spendthrift and tightwad scenario and how it may be resolved. Now, let's address the mechanics of money-handling. There's no one right and true way to handle money, and whatever works for you is fine. However, I must say it raises red warning flags in my mind when I hear couples talking about "your money" and "my money." I've known couples who successfully kept their money rigidly separate and distinct for years. Each spouse was responsible for his or her personal bills, and they negotiated over payment of mutual expenses such as the house note, utilities, and food. Each was then free to spend what was left over on whatever they liked. I've seen this work out quite harmoniously for some couples. It especially seems appropriate for second marriages or marriages contracted later in life, where both spouses may have accumulated considerable independent estates, retirement accounts, etc. prior to the marriage.

Nonetheless, I find this approach inappropriate and even potentially dangerous for most marriages. It is simply antithetical to the spirit of team play which is essential to marital success. It encourages the two partners to act independently, in their own interests rather than that of the marriage. It tends to encourage greediness, short-term spending instead of saving, and continued conflict over finances. It's cumbersome, inefficient, even expensive to maintain two checking accounts, separate bank cards, etc. Quoting Bonnie Raitt again, "You can't have love, children, when you're keeping score." Keeping separate finances tends to lead to a lot of score-keeping and comparing. I paid for this while you only paid for that. It tends to produce a spirit of independent or even selfish use of money. It can even lead to dishonesty, as one spouse tries to hide money from the other. It also seems to me artificial, even unrealistic. Could you have a marriage in which the husband lived in luxury while the wife lived in poverty? Would she have to rent space in his mansion? What if she couldn't afford to live there? Can she watch his big-screen TV , or does she have to settle for the used black-and-white in her nasty little bedroom, sitting on a mattress on the floor because she can't afford a bed? Since our society compensates men more lavishly for the same work, this approach to marital finances ensures that most women will be at a disadvantage to their husbands. It also means financial matters must be renegotiated constantly, as the spouses' jobs, salaries or needs change.

Keeping the money rigidly separate tends to lead to power struggles and inappropriate control of one spouse over the other. In one-income families it can produce a situation in which *all* money is considered to be the husband's, in which the wife has to ask for anything she needs, in which all control is in the hands of the husband. While some couples are happy with this arrangement, it seems to me unfair and probably dysfunctional for most.

I think a better approach is some variation on the "one-pot" theory. This approach assumes that all assets are held in common, that it's one for all and all for one. Any income produced by either partner goes into a common pot. Any money spent by either comes out of the pot. All of it is "our" money, and there's no comparison of the different amounts contributed. Funds are expended only when both spouses agree on the purchase. In a one-income marriage the same rules apply. In either a one or two- income family all contributions to the family's welfare are gratefully accepted and valued, whether monetary or otherwise, without comparison, judging, or keeping score of who does what. One spouse may contribute more money while the other contributes more child care, house-cleaning, bill-paying, etc. But it's all still going into and coming out of the same one pot. I couldn't make as much money as I do if you weren't taking care of the kids and keeping the home fires burning. It's a team effort and both should share equally in the benefits.

Like all systems, this one has pros and cons, but I think the advantages outweigh the disadvantages, especially with a few modifications. The one-pot system emphasizes cooperation, sharing, equality, and joint decision-making. It encourages long-term planning and saving, because it disallows impulsive spending. It encourages personal sacrifice for the good of the family because it values all contributions. It simplifies bookkeeping and eliminates the need for negotiating and contracting to determine who pays what. There's no need for keeping score because everything is done by and for the team.

The one-pot system is not without its drawbacks, but I think they are manageable. One is that it demands a consensus between the spouses before any money can be spent. While it's useful to force the two to come to terms with each other, it can also lead to more conflict, and it certainly can slow down their response time. Another drawback is that this system may feel pretty confining and controlling, especially to the spouse who's more inclined to spend freely. "I'm a grown man, I work hard, and I make a good living," he may argue. "Why do I have to get Mommy's permission to spend my own money?" The answer, of course, is that it isn't *his* money, it's *their* money. Nonetheless, I'm sympathetic to his complaint. It doesn't feel right to ask for permission to buy something. My wife and I found an easy solution to this problem: We've agreed on a set amount either of us can spend on a whim, without consultation or permission from the other. The figure has gone up a bit as our incomes have, but neither of us spends more than the set amount without checking it out with the other. If I happen across a nice shirt at the mall, I can plop down my forty bucks and carry it home. The thousand-dollar suit requires the wife's advice and consent, even if it's a real bargain. This system allows me enough independence and spontaneity not to feel controlled or constrained, yet ensures that I won't spend *our* money in ways *we* don't agree on. I've occasionally had to wait for my purchase to work its way to the top of our priority list, and the antique Chinese clock never did. I consider it a small price to pay for marital harmony. I also don't have to feel guilty when I do make a purchase, because we've agreed it's okay.

As to the mechanics of the system, we have numerous credit cards, some in her name, some in mine. All get paid off monthly, out of the same account. We have one checking account, which my wife keeps in balance. My job is to record my checks and hers is to reconcile my book to the master checkbook. By law retirement accounts are separate, but both are assumed to be community property.

Household Duties:

Until recently most people grew up in traditional families where Dad went to work and Mom stayed home to take care of the house and the kids. We come into our own marriages expecting things to be pretty much the same way. Most of us, however, find ourselves in marriages where both spouses are employed outside the home. For most of us it is simply not economically feasible for the wife to stay at home, at least not if we desire to match or exceed our parents' standard of living. This means something has got to give, and it's usually our traditional model of marriage.

It just isn't fair or realistic to expect a woman to work forty-plus hours a week on the job, then come home and do all the child care, all the cooking, and all the house-cleaning. If both spouses are working, they should split the housework evenly, including child care. This means negotiating who does what and doing your part faithfully. It means guys will need to learn how to cook, mop, and diaper, and some gals may need to learn how to change the oil in the car. They'll probably both be better people for it, though they won't necessarily like it. Certainly it's okay to assign chores to the one best able to do them, and this will often mean traditional gender-based roles. But if *all* chores are so divided, it's almost certain the wife is over-loaded and the husband isn't doing his fair share.

Unfortunately, research indicates this is exactly what is happening. On the average, women are employed outside the home and doing most of the housework as well. Men are doing more home and child care than they used to, but in most families it's still less than 50 per cent. This puts a real strain on the wife and ultimately on the marriage as well. Ironically, Women's Liberation has made it possible to develop an executive ulcer while preserving your housemaid's knees.

Again, **what is called for here is a spirit of team play and a willingness to make sacrifices for the good of the family, without keeping score.** Forget about how your parents did things, be flexible, and look at what works best in *your* family. If Mom clocks in at eight o'clock sharp but Dad's hours are more flexible, let him carpool the kids. If Mom's home at five, but Dad doesn't roll in until six-thirty, she can cook during the week and he can do the dishes and clean up the kitchen. He can cook more on weekends. It's okay for the husband to handle the yard work and the wife the decorating, if those are their preferences and talents. Past a certain point, however, gardening and sprucing up the house are hobbies and don't count as chores. When times change, be prepared to change with them and switch roles as needed. By the way, kids should have chores, too, and right from the toddler stage. But that's a topic for another book.

Men should also share and participate in all aspects of child care as well. With the exception of breast-feeding there's very little basis for splitting up parenting duties according to gender. If the baby is on formula, Dad's just as well equipped to handle the two a.m. feeding as Mom is. I suppose playing catch with the boys might be another exception, although my housekeeper Emma is a considerably better pitcher than I am. Sharing child care more or less equally is not only fair, it's usually better parenting. I strongly encourage fathers to take care of their babies, right from the beginning. In so doing they establish a mutual bond and a nurturing relationship which will form the loving basis for the discipline that comes later. They will overcome their fear of babies and learn to develop the loving, nurturing side of their own personalities. They will earn the respect and appreciation of their wives. A man is never more masculine than when he is acting in the role of father, even taking care of a baby, no matter what he has been taught to see as "macho."

Similarly, I encourage mothers to discipline their children, partly to provide balanced parenting, partly to develop the strong side of their own personality, and partly because most women are frequently called upon to discipline without a man's help. "Wait until your father gets home" not only sets Dad up to be the heavy; it also undercuts Mom's own authority. It's an admission of incompetence. Your husband should provide back-up support, not replace you on the front line. You, of course, should reinforce his discipline as well. If he's too harsh or seems unfair, discuss it with him away from the children. You must maintain a united front, and this is easier when both parents are fully involved in all aspects of parenting.

Sex:

Many marital conflicts about sex are really just power struggles with the bed arbitrarily chosen as the battleground. They could as easily be fighting about kids or money– and probably are. Others are more properly considered differences about intimacy, with problems around emotional as well as physical closeness. Other conflicts represent differences in levels of desire, preferred frequency, sexual practices and particular likes and dislikes, or about who is to initiate sex. What, where, when, why and whom are all fair grounds for dispute. In any case, conflicts over sex tend to be especially delicate, sensitive, and volatile. They go to the heart of the marital relationship, and they must be resolved if the marriage is to last.

Women are sometimes surprised to find how important sex is to their husbands. Men are often surprised to find how important their emotional relationship is to their wives, and therefore to their own sex lives. Granted, a true marriage is a wedding together of soulmates, but sexual desire is part of what first attracted them and a major part of the bond that holds a couple together. "Making love" really does tend to generate and sustain loving feelings. And, as we've noted before, not being sexually fulfilled tends to make people grumpy and irritable, especially men.

The range of normal sexual habits is a wide one. Thus, it is common for two entirely normal mates to develop conflicts around their mating preferences. As in other areas of marital functioning, it isn't especially useful to set standards, compare yourselves to others, or assume that there are absolute rights and wrongs. Whatever is mutually satisfying is fine. Some couples, especially young and newly married ones, have sex every day. Some, especially older ones, have sex once a month or less. Both are normal. For what it's worth, "average" is probably about twice a week. Problems arise when one spouse desires sex much more frequently than the other. Similarly, conflicts develop when one partner is very conservative or even puritanical and the other likes to experiment with the kinky stuff. Mutual respect and consideration, a willingness to try different things, and compromise are essential to resolving these differences.

It is quite helpful if you and your mate can talk about the problem. Unfortunately, many married people cannot. Sex is too personal, too sensitive, too biological for many people to discuss, especially with someone with whom they share a bed and a marriage. It's too embarrassing, so they avoid the issue and hope it will all go away. Eventually it *will* go away, but the marriage is likely to go with it. As an extreme example, a patient once told me that he and his wife had been unable to consummate their marriage on the honeymoon. Both were virgins and utterly naive as to sex, and they just couldn't figure out how to make connections. They were so humiliated by this failure that they never tried again, and neither mentioned it for ten years. The wife finally got so frustrated she found another man to show her how to do it. The husband eventually found a girlfriend who showed him. Unfortunately, when he returned to share his new knowledge with his wife, she'd run off with her instructor. If only they could have talked about their sex problem, perhaps with a counselor or physician, they'd have saved ten years of misery and probably their marriage.

The first step in resolving sexual difficulties is to learn to talk openly and freely about them. A good marriage counselor or sex therapist can help a lot.

You must be able to say what you do and don't like, what your desires are, what you're uncomfortable with or find immoral. It would be nice if you both simply *knew* how to please each other. Many people assume that their mate can essentially read their mind and, if their spouse truly loves them, they will automatically know what to do. Unfortunately, this is not the case. You can get a long way in simply observing your partner's nonverbal behavior, noticing what seems to be a turn-on or a turn-off. But, as we've seen earlier, there's plenty of room for misinterpreting nonverbal messages. For some people, talking about what you like sexually, spoils the romance. Maybe it's not quite as good to get what you need by asking for it, instead of your partner magically knowing and supplying it. But it's "good enough," and a lot better than being frustrated and upset.

I usually advise couples to be open-minded and flexible and to take an experimental approach to sex. Try doing things a bit differently and look at the results. Keep doing what you both like. Don't be too hasty to reject a new position, technique, or whatever. You probably didn't like oysters or olives the first time either. If there's something you're not especially wild about (say, oral sex or perhaps some weird position) but it doesn't disgust or embarrass you, do it out of love for your partner. On the other hand, if there's something your spouse really dislikes, don't pressure him or her to engage in this practice. There are plenty of other alternatives. Over all, remember that sex is a loving communication, not just the meeting of a biological need. It should be done lovingly.

This doesn't mean it need always be done romantically or even passionately. Sex can also be done playfully, gently, or just routinely and still feel good. If one partner isn't in the mood, he or she should not be coerced or made to feel guilty for an occasional no. On the other hand, it's also quite acceptable to do it anyway, just to be nice to the one you love.

Most couples should expect their sex lives to change over the years, as aging, responsibilities, and children take their toll. Declining interest and decreased frequency are pretty normal in stressed-out adults and should not be taken as a personal rejection. Children are inconvenient in a multitude of ways, and amongst these is their interference with your sex life. Babies tend to be awake when you want to be asleep or in need of feeding, changing, or rocking when you'd prefer to be rock- and- rolling with each other. The sheer exhaustion and sleep-deprivation of parenting an infant is enough to kill your sex life temporarily. Having a toddler in your bed takes the edge off a romantic interlude. Parents of older kids may be limited to sneaking in a "quickie" between ballet delivery and soccer pick-up. Mutual consideration and adaptability, as well as some resourcefulness, are helpful.

Men hit their sexual peak at about nineteen years and often taper off some in middle age. Women tend to peak a lot later, at around forty or so. This means there's often a significant discrepancy between their levels of interest and capacity, and this can be frustrating to both. After about the age of forty, men tend to produce male hormones primarily when they engage in intercourse. These hormones determine both their level of desire and their level of performance. If they stop having sex very much, they may begin to lose both interest as well as ability. It's a use it or lose it proposition. As in other areas of marital life, mutual respect, sensitivity and willingness to compromise are essential to working out these differences. A sense of humor doesn't hurt either.

Surprisingly few couples come to me with a presenting complaint about sex. When they do it's almost always clear that the sexual problem is secondary to a relationship problem. In fact, the sexual dysfunction often resolves spontaneously when the relationship is repaired. In any case, sexual problems are best dealt with in the context of the relationship per se, as Masters and Johnson discovered. I have, however, seen absolutely horrible marriages that were kept together by great sex. These couples were generally quite impaired interpersonally and able to relate effectively only in terms of sexual intimacy and excitement. They hated each other but stayed together because this was the only closeness they were capable of. I usually advise them to divorce before they kill each other, perhaps date each other occasionally, and both get into individual psychotherapy.

This is admittedly a pretty cursory discussion of an area of marital life as broad and important as sex. The same rules apply here as in other areas: opposites attract; learn to value your spouse's way of being; work respectfully towards a mutually satisfactory resolution to your differences. There's one other problem in this area that should be addressed, though it may strike some readers as an uncommon one. This is the problem of childhood sexual abuse and its impact on later marital functioning. Unfortunately, this is not an uncommon problem at all, as research indicates that some thirty to forty per cent of women in our society, and perhaps twenty per cent of men, have been sexually abused at some time in their early years.

Sexual Abuse and Its Effects on Marriage:

Childhood or adolescent sexual abuse can and often does have an enormous and long-lasting effect on its victims. Sexual abuse makes children feel ashamed, unloved, and disgusting. It ravages their self-esteem and does so specifically in terms of their gender identities and ability to relate to the opposite sex. A little girl who is sexually abused feels badly about herself as a female. A little boy who is sexually abused may not even be able to see himself as male. Sexual abuse leads to tremendous fear and mistrust in relating to persons of the opposite sex, yet also imparts a powerful yearning to be loved and validated by one. Sexually molested girls learn to relate to men sexually, and they crave a man's love and approval. Consequently, they sometimes end up in a series of promiscuous, abusive relationships with men who "love" them and leave them, adding to their fear and shame. They may also have significant difficulty in relating sexually in a marriage, feeling "used" or "cheap" or doubting their husband's love.

Childhood sexual abuse can leave behind a residue of emotions, behaviors, and ways of relating that are highly destructive to a marriage. Sexual dysfunction is at high risk from the start. Mistrust, suspiciousness, and an inexplicable fear of intimacy are also likely. Victims of abuse tend to marry abusers, unconsciously repeating their early history; some even act in ways calculated to induce abuse. For example, they may express anger in passive-aggressive ways, which is infuriating and invites an aggressive retaliation. Unaware of the underlying cause, perplexed spouses find themselves rejected, falsely accused or acting in ways they don't understand themselves. (Refer to our earlier discussion of the Cycle of Abuse.)

Fortunately, these problems can usually be dealt with very effectively in marital and/or individual therapy. It may take a long time, even several years, to repair the damage of childhood sexual abuse, and it can be a very painful process. However, just getting it out in the open and identifying the real problem, then dealing with it together, can begin a couple's process of healing. This kind of work is difficult, but the results can be most gratifying. I've often been impressed by the courage victims show in dealing with their abuse, as well as the loyalty and steadfastness they find in their spouses.

Dependency:

I sometimes shock my patients by telling them that my wife doesn't need me. But it is quite true. Oh, granted, she needs companionship, she needs a financial partner, she needs someone to father her children and to be intimate with. She needs all the things all people need from a marriage. The point is that she could get all these needs met from another person or persons. She doesn't specifically need *me.* Actually, she's quite capable of doing most things for herself. When I met her she was living independently, working full time and putting herself through a second graduate program, not to mention a second corneal transplant. She was independent, self-reliant and happy; that's why I was attracted to her. What she couldn't do for herself she could get done. Actually, I didn't need her either, though I definitely wanted her.

My wife doesn't need me, and that's just the way I like it. Though independent and able to meet all her needs elsewhere, she comes home to me. She comes freely, voluntarily, because she doesn't have to. If she desperately needed me, she'd have no choice. That makes me feel good. I'd a lot rather be wanted than needed.

Pop culture confuses love and dependency, and many people can't distinguish them. "I need you, I want you, I love you ," say the pop songs, as if those three things were synonymous. But they aren't. To want someone is to desire to be with that person. It involves a positive, attractive force that draws persons together on a voluntary, even enthusiastic basis. In extreme form it can become obsessive, a desire to possess another, whether emotionally or sexually. At that level, wanting becomes a kind of addiction that is exciting and flattering, but not the basis for a long-term relationship. In normal limits, it is simply a desire for a mutually loving relationship. To love someone is to accept, to value, to share with and to be committed to that person. To need someone is to be dependent on him or her, in some way, to be unable to survive without that person. It is based on a deficiency, if not a frank pathology. This, too, can be flattering for a while, but eventually it tends to become quite bothersome, if not burdensome.

A high level of dependency is generally a bad sign in a marriage, even when the dependency is mutual. It's okay to depend on somebody temporarily, but it creates problems in long-term relationships, because it inherently involves some degree of coerciveness and control. If I truly need you, cannot survive without you, depend utterly on you, then I automatically put you in a bind. You must either take care of me or feel guilty for refusing to do so. You may not like this choice and may feel controlled by my dependency. On the other hand, if I truly need you, then you have control over me, too.

You agree to take care of me, but only if we do things your way. After all, how else could you take care of me but your way? Well, I may like being taken care of, but I don't like you telling me what to do.

Unfortunately, it's a package deal. Dependency inherently means control, and control leads to resentment. I once met a woman who'd been so dependent on her ex-husband that she didn't know how to wind or set her own watch. At first he'd felt very flattered by this. What a strong, capable guy he was! Eventually it became simply a suffocating burden. He got sick of doing everything for her and dumped her for a more independent woman. I taught her to set the watch and recommended she learn to take care of herself.

I'm seeing a couple in which the wife is unhappy because her husband doesn't take care of her like her father did. In fact, she's a bright, capable person who can take of herself, something he's always found attractive in her. She became even more independent as he spent long hours in graduate school and in starting his career. But she misses the feelings she had as a little girl, feelings she expected to get from her husband. Because she no longer "needs" him, she feels she doesn't love him, and she doesn't feel loved by him. Further, she's aware that he derives most of his happiness from her and their daughter, and this makes her feel suffocated. She can't see that he's making himself happy with her and she needn't do anything to take care of him.

Instead, she needs to be making herself happy with him. I'm seeing another couple who've been having an affair for years. She divorced, but he never seems to be able to end his marriage for her, partly because his extremely dependent wife (who knows about the affair) threatens suicide if he starts talking divorce. The girlfriend has moved to be with him, works for him, has given up her family and friends for him, and has loaned him tens of thousands of dollars. She knows he is lying to her and using her. Yet she is so dependent on him she can't imagine living without him. Everyone has advised her to leave, including me. But she can't decide to go. In fact, she's trying to get *him* to make the decision and tell her what to do! This incredibly sick relationship involves pathological dependency all around. The man has two women utterly dependent on him emotionally, yet he is unable to take any responsibility and owes his paramour money. It is a striking testimony to the problems of dependency in marriage.

Dependency unbalances a relationship and puts one partner in a one-up position. It leads to control and resentment. What is the alternative? In healthy marriages there is what might be called "mutual interdependency." The two agree to rely on each other for certain things and to meet each other's needs. It's all voluntary, however, and in theory each could meet his or her needs elsewhere or for themselves. When I was single I kept my own bank book and did my own taxes. I didn't like it and wasn't particularly good at it, but I did it, and I could do it again. Now my wife handles the finances, because she's excellent at it and even kind of likes it. I rely on her for this, but I could do it if I had to. She relies on me to mow the lawn (a chore that's actually an enjoyable break for me from listening to people all day). My wife couldn't mow it herself, because the lot's too hilly, but she could easily afford to pay for a lawn service. **We depend on each other, but it's equal, balanced and voluntary. That's mutual interdependency.**

Of course, in order to establish this kind of marriage, both partners must be relatively independent and self-reliant coming into it or pretty quickly get that way. This is one reason why people who marry very young have difficulty making it work. They haven't had a chance yet to learn how to take care of themselves and make themselves happy, so they look to each other to do so, establishing very dependent relationships. I strongly encourage young people to grow up first, live on their own for a while, and then think about getting married. I think it's particularly important for women, both in terms of their independence and in terms of their identity. Most women these days will be employed outside the home and most will be divorced or widowed at some point in their lives. They need to know how to take care of themselves in the world. They'll also make better marriages and have more power in their relationships if they learn to be more independent. A period of independent living is also important in terms of identity development. Many women grow up thinking of themselves as somebody's daughter, somebody's sister, somebody's girlfriend, then somebody's wife. They define themselves relative to others, finally becoming identified in their own minds as somebody's mother. They never see themselves simply as *somebody*, in their own right. Independent living gives them this valuable experience.

The most destructive of dependent marriages is the co-dependent one, of which the prototype is the alcoholic marriage. Alcoholics are dependent people. They depend on alcohol to deal with their feelings and they depend on their spouses to roll them into bed, bail them out of jail, and to make excuses to the boss for their absences. Alcoholics need alcohol and an enabling spouse. Spouses of alcoholics need to be needed. That's the *co-*dependency. As we've seen earlier, codependent people derive their self-esteem and seek to be happy in life by taking care of needy people. The trouble is, their care-taking facilitates the alcoholic's drinking, keeping both of them unhealthy and unhappy.

There are marriages in which a high degree of dependency is unavoidable, and these aren't necessarily bad or unhealthy marriages. Indeed, they are often very good ones. My cotherapist in Austin, for example, had been crippled by childhood polio and was bound to an electric wheelchair. She had limited use of her arms and hands, no use of her legs, but a keen mind and a good sense of humor. She was a powerful, talented therapist. She was married to an able-bodied and loving man for whom she had bourne two children. Her physical dependency on him was nearly complete, yet they seemed to be quite happily married, and they functioned very much as equal partners. Her physical needs were just a part of the bargain that both understood and accepted from the beginning. There didn't seem to be any pity or control on his part. In fact, he and the kids both knew to behave themselves, for this lady was a power to be feared if crossed. Actor Christopher Reeve was transformed in a riding accident from the movies' Superman to a complete quadriplegic. He is utterly dependent on his wife, a radical change in their relationship. Yet media accounts indicate they are doing well.

Why do these marriages prosper despite the problem of dependency? Perhaps one reason is that in both of these cases the "dependent" spouse is also extremely bright, talented, strong-willed, and capable within their limitations. Both are as independent as they can be and both have found ways to be truly productive contributors to the marriage and to society. I never had the feeling that my friend was helpless, weak, or incompetent. Similarly, though totally paralyzed, Mr. Reeve has successfully undertaken a whole new career as advocate and fund-raiser for people with spinal chord injuries. He is still a powerful and capable and productive man. He even acts on occasion.

Divorce, Remarriage, and Step-parenting:

While this is a book about being happy, and more specifically about marital happiness, our discussion of marriage is incomplete without a quick look at divorce, remarriage, and step-families. When people are unhappy in their marriages they tend to see divorce as a way to restore happiness in their lives. This undoubtedly works out fine for some, but others will be greatly disappointed and may end up unhappier than ever. Remarriage often lands people in the same old situation, only with a new partner. And step-families have a whole set of problems all their own, in addition to the usual ones.

Divorce is typically horrible for children and not all that good for grown-ups. I've actually recommended divorce on a few occasions, but I usually advise couples to stay together and work things out if they possibly can. For children divorce is often experienced as the death of a parent. Many will literally never see their father (or mother) again, once the divorce papers are signed. If you have kids, divorce doesn't end your relationship with your spouse, it just changes it. The old problems and bad feelings are still there and the conflicts unresolved. On top of these is the additional anger and bitterness generated by the process of divorcing itself. Only now all you have to fight about is child support payments and visitation schedules. This puts the children squarely in the middle of the continuing battle between their parents. Research shows that this is the key determinant of children's adjustment to divorce. If the parents can either quit fighting, or at least remove the children from the battleground, the kids will eventually adjust pretty well. If the kids are stuck in the middle, they will continue to have problems. Unfortunately, while I've seen several "friendly" divorces, they are the exception, not the rule.

Divorce is an emotional roller-coaster, and people act in cruel and crazy ways they wouldn't dream of at other times. Children see all this, including a lot they shouldn't even be aware of. I've talked to many children who have seen their fathers drive through the front yard, shooting into the mother's home. I've seen others who were kidnaped by one parent and hidden from the other, and I've talked with kids who walked in on their mother and her boyfriend in the shower. Divorce puts children in all sorts of inappropriate, difficult, even abusive situations. It profoundly changes their lives and their relationships with their parents. It demands many difficult adjustments and adaptations. For many children divorce means adjusting to a new home, changing to a new school, leaving long-time buddies, rarely seeing Dad, coming home alone, and learning to live with a new set of step-parents and siblings. It typically involves a sizable drop in economic status, at least temporarily. It usually results in the child getting a lot less parenting and it often ends up with the child taking care of the troubled adults. Divorce destroys your image of who your family is and, often, your self-esteem as well. Divorce has little to offer children unless it gets them out of a highly conflictual home.

Adults don't always fare that well either. Most are amazed at the intensity and volatility of their own emotions, as they swing rapidly from joyfulness to rage, relief to depression. If marriage is the creation of a new psycho-biological entity, divorce is the death of it. It demands a lot of grieving– for lost love, lost companionship, the loss of an intact family, even the loss of the fantasies of what might have been. Growing old together, retiring to a life of shared ease, rocking on the porch, or perhaps traveling to see the grandkids– all of this is lost and must be mourned. Most divorcing people feel like failures and suffer a loss of self-esteem as well. It can be terrifying to face the world on your own again, perhaps for the rest of your life. The prospect of dating again has its own peculiar horrors, especially in the AIDS era. Many divorcees doubt they'll ever be able to trust again, though most do.

Most divorced people remarry, often surprisingly fast. Many of them realize that they like being married and miss it, even if they don't miss who they were married to. The general rule of thumb is that you're not emotionally ready for a serious relationship for a couple of years after a divorce, but most people can't wait that long. Women often find men "hitting on" them before the court date is on the docket, seeing them as easy targets. They're lonely and hurt and they're used to an active sex life, so they're vulnerable. Tragically, these men are too often correct, and many recent divorcees find themselves used, rejected, and abandoned again. Some grow increasingly bitter and mistrustful of all men.

Psychologically speaking, adjusting to divorce means disconnecting emotionally from your ex-, learning to see him or her as single, separate, and just another human being to be dealt with more or less like anyone else. This is why I tell divorced people to relate to their exes as one would in a business relationship. More particularly, relate as you would in doing business with someone you don't particularly like. Keep it emotionally cool (but not cold), businesslike, and polite; avoid anything which could lead to conflict or controversy. It's really in everybody's best interest to stick to the business at hand and relate cooperatively and considerately. Avoid hatred or bitterness, as these will maintain the emotional connection you are trying to sever. In fact, hatred can be a more intimate, intense, and lasting bond than love. When you're able to achieve this emotional adjustment, you're ready for a new relationship. Until that time, you're likely to conduct a new relationship in terms of the old one, rather than on its own basis. You'll either keep picking the same kind of person for a mate or swing to an equally inappropriate opposite.

Courtship tends to be a fairly crazy time in most people's lives, a time of great joy, great anxiety, impulsive acting-out and obsession with the object of one's desires. Ordinarily all this silliness happens long before kids come onto the scene. Divorced kids, unfortunately, see it all, from moonlight dancing to frantic phone calls to gooey poetry. Can you still respect a Dad who mopes about like a lovesick fool? Can you feel secure with a Mom who breaks down in tears twice daily? There are issues of sexual morality to be considered, often involving a double standard for parents and teens. There's also the problem of children becoming attached to the parents' new partners and suffering another loss when the partnership breaks up (as most dating relationships inevitably will.) For all these reasons, I advise dating divorcees to shield their children as much as possible by keeping their romances away from the kids, especially at first. There's a natural tendency to begin doing things as a family with your new boyfriend or girlfriend, especially if there are kids on both sides. For one thing, it solves the childcare problem, as well as giving you back that good family feeling. A bit of this is okay, but I'd avoid getting the kids too involved until the relationship begins to look more permanent. This protects the kids from repeated hurts and allows the new relationship to develop more naturally, on a one-to-one basis, as it should. I've seen people remarry because their kids loved the new boy or girlfriend and became close to his or her kids, only to realize later that *they* weren't really in love at all.

At some point it is necessary for kids and prospective new spouses to meet and develop some kind of relationship. There's no guarantee that your

kids will like someone just because you do. While
you can't very well let your kids pick your spouse
(though some folks do) you'd also be properly
reluctant to rush into marriage with somebody they
can't stand. The same holds for their new step-
siblings. There are many reasons why kids may be
likely *not* to approve of your new choice in partners.
They may see him as an interloper intruding into
their private lives without invitation. They may see
her as an evil woman who stole Daddy, hurt
Mommy, and broke up their family. They may see
the new mate as a rival for a parent's affections, as
someone who takes Mommy away from them or is
trying to take over as Daddy's replacement. They are
likely to resent the time dating takes you away from
them, and take it out on the new spouse. And they
may not cotton at all to the notion of sharing their
bedroom with some creepy new kid they barely
know.

Remarriage is a very risky proposition and should
be entered into cautiously, slowly, with eyes wide
open. Second and later marriages have a higher
divorce rate than first marriages, partly because
people aren't learning from their mistakes, and partly
because stepfamilies are extremely hard to do. We
have few cultural models for step-parents, and most
of them are negative (Cinderella's cruel stepmother
and stepsisters, for example.) Second marriages
must bear up under all the baggage of mistrust,
betrayal, blown self-esteem, and bitterness dragged
in from the first one. The ex- must be dealt with,

especially if there are kids, and visitation and support issues can be terribly draining on a new marriage. There may be considerable resistance to the new marriage from in-laws and friends. Some may even openly refuse to accept the new spouse or bless the new marriage. Ordinarily you get a bit of a honeymoon before parenting must be dealt with, but not so in a second marriage. It's much harder to handle the developmental challenges of making a new marriage when the relationship is entangled with child issues right from the start. It's hard to bond properly when you don't have much time alone together.

Most troublesome of all, remarriages are risky and unstable by their very nature. The marriage is the primary relationship in a family, the core around which the family is built. The marital relationship is the primary commitment. Kids are in a sense "temps," coming after the marriage is formed and (hopefully) leaving one day to form families of their own. In a sense, you'd choose your spouse over your kids, if push came to shove. In effect, you do, as you stay with each other when the kids have departed. Remarriages turn this picture entirely on its ear: here the primary, pre-existing, and predominant relationship is between parent and child, with the marriage secondary. Not only does this elevate the child to a dangerously inappropriate level of power and importance, it stresses the new marriage tremendously. People naturally want to be first in the heart of their mate, but in a second marriage, you're not. You may find yourself jealous of your stepchildren. You may find your house taken over and your spouse's total attention devoted to undisciplined, spoiled, and disrespectful kids who are actively sabotaging your new marriage. No wonder stepfamilies often degenerate into two hostile camps, with you and your kids lined up to do battle with me and mine.

Remarriages and stepfamilies are no picnic for the kids, either. There's often another relocation, perhaps also another school to contend with. Or perhaps you stay put but suddenly must share *your room* with a brat you just met, at least on alternate weekends. Not only do you see Mom less, but your new "Dad"-- who never threw you a baseball or bought you a toy doll house– thinks you're spoiled and is determined to whip you into shape. You didn't pick this guy, Mom did; but you're expected to love, respect, and obey him. It's even worse for teenagers who are busily trying to divest themselves of the parents they already have. The last thing they want is a new Mom or Dad to tell them what to do. Step-parents find themselves dealing with highly rebellious and resentful children, often without any support from their spouse. Indeed, I often see spouses actively undercutting the authority of their mates and colluding in the rebellion of their children, either seeing their mate as too harsh, or perhaps as part of their own power struggle.

There's also a major problem of divided loyalties, often exacerbated by mixed feelings about natural parents. Children, especially younger ones, often find the whole step- business pretty confusing and sometimes threatening. Lines of authority are vague, people in the same family have different surnames, and it's hard to sort out who's related to whom. Half-siblings complicate things further when they come along. I've seen a family with six people who had five different last names. *I* couldn't sort out the relationships or keep track of who belonged to who, and I'm sure the kids were hopelessly lost. I've seen children very upset at Mom's remarriage because they thought this turned their natural father into a stepfather. Children get very contradictory messages about how to relate to step-parents and may experience very divided loyalties. Mom demands they love or at least respect their new stepfather, but Dad may be displeased if they do so. He may even be bad-mouthing the guy and insisting the kids defy his authority. Many children end up trying to choose who to displease. You can't afford to have Dad mad at you, since you rarely see him anyway, and if he's angry he may stop seeing you altogether. On the other hand, you have to *live* with Mom and her husband. It's often worse when the natural father is mean or neglectful, rarely sees his kids, or breaks his promises of trips, toys, etc. If step-Dad's a pretty good guy, the child may find that he loves his new father better than the old. This can greatly intensify his fear of total abandonment by his natural father, as well as inducing tremendous guilt feelings. Some kids will reject the stepfather to avoid this emotional conflict, even if it means hanging on to a father who mistreats them or to the mere fantasy of an absent father.

Step-families are almost ideally suited for bad parenting. Not only does the child experience two different households, with two different sets of rules, but the animosity stirred up by the divorce usually ensures a continued battle between them. Kids get crushed in-between, but also have endless opportunities to manipulate and "split" their parents. Dad becomes a playmate who doesn't discipline at all, and Mom may be too tired or too depressed. Adding step-parents tends to exacerbate and complicate the problem. Now there are four parents to disagree on how to deal with the kids, and two of them are coming from an entirely new perspective. Step-parents often step into a fairly chaotic situation and tend to see the kids as out of control. They view their job as jumping in to clean up the mess, and they begin to discipline with a vengeance. The children resent this and see it as simply mean, especially since they do not have the "normal" experience of growing up with this parent. The heavy nurturing comes early in the child's life and serves as a basis and background for the discipline that comes later. But step-parents lack this early base of nurturing as a context for their discipline. Thus, their efforts to discipline seem abusive and unfair to the stepchild. Step-parents may also be inclined to exercise discipline differently with their own kids, furthering the stepchild's resentment. Step-kids rebel, complain to natural parents, and begin to split the new couple apart.

Adjusting to divorce can take years and lead to a lot of problems. Adults and children commonly experience high levels of anxiety, as well as serious clinical depressions. Job or school performance may suffer, friends may be lost, and fatigue is a nearly constant factor for some. Five years after their parents' divorce, half of the kids in one study were still in distress and still harbored fantasies of reconciling their parents. Like most therapists, I find my caseload heavily over-balanced in the direction of divorced people. Most of the kids I see are from divorced families.

There are also many individuals and families who adjust fairly easily and quickly to divorce. Some end up a lot better off then they were before. For some children divorce removes them from a highly conflictual and tense family and ultimately places them in a loving, cooperative one. A fair number of divorced couples rediscover that they make pretty good friends, even if pretty lousy mates. I used to treat a child whose natural parents had both been married and divorced several times, but who got along quite famously with all of them. In fact *all* the parents, step-parents, and ex-step-parents came to his baseball games, sat together and cheered as a block. This is exceptional, of course, but cordial and cooperative exes are not. Divorce offers the possibility– indeed it demands it– of individual growth. Many highly dependent and unhappy people learn to take care of themselves and really fulfill themselves for the first time, after a divorce.

If you are unhappily married, find a good therapist and do all you can to work it out. If there is any possible way, get your spouse to go with you to counseling. If none of this is effective and you must divorce, here are some guidelines to follow:

1. Get a good, tough, but fair attorney to represent your interests within the parameters you set. An attorney represents only the person who pays the fee, so don't try to get by cheaply by sharing one with your spouse. Divorce is an adversarial process, by law, so you need someone to look after your best interests. However, the divorce process stirs up enough animosity as is, so it's usually not a good idea to "go for blood." Remember, you'll have to relate to your ex- for a long time to come.

2. Try to maintain cordial, considerate, cooperative, but emotionally cool relationship with your ex-spouse. It's now a business relationship, so stick to business, keep it unemotional, and try to get along. This will best serve your interests and those of your children.

3. Divorce adjustment is quicker and easier if you have a good support system of friends and family. In addition, or as an alternative, divorce adjustment groups can be very helpful and supportive. Many churches and counseling centers offer them at little or no cost.

4. A good therapist or counselor can also provide

very helpful guidance and moral support, as well as helping you sort out what went wrong and what you need to avoid in your next marriage.

5. Psychologically, your job is to disconnect emotionally from your ex- and re-establish yourself as an independent, self-reliant person. Avoid conflict and dependency. In particular, don't lean on your children too much. You must maintain a position of authority, and that's hard to do when you're crying on your nine-year-old's shoulder.

6. Try to keep as much as possible to the children's old routines and minimize changes for them. Continue to be a parent and follow the rules. Don't be just a buddy or over-utilize your kids as compatriots. Discipline consistently.

7. Try to keep your ex-spouse involved with you in parenting. Respect his or her authority and house rules. Don't bad-mouth or down-rate your ex- to your kids.

8. Be slow to date and slower yet to marry. It takes two or more years to get over a divorce and be ready for a new relationship. Don't involve the kids too quickly with your new partners. If you've been having an affair, take even longer and think even harder before marrying. Marrying your paramour doesn't absolve you of guilt for the affair, and such marriages are highly unlikely to succeed.

9. Place your new marriage at the center of your new family instead of making the parent-child relationship primary. Take time alone as a couple, and work on your relationship. Insist the children

respect their new step-parent's authority. Be fair and loving with your new stepchildren.

10. Keep an open mind, be flexible, compromise, and be ready to grow and adapt. It's a whole new ball game out there.

Making a Happy Marriage:

The foregoing discussion should be enough to demonstrate that making a happy marriage isn't automatic and isn't always easy. It requires effort, a willingness to communicate, to compromise, to grow, and to make sacrifices. But it isn't all just work, either. **Marriage is the deepest, most intimate, and most rewarding relationship in most of our lives.** It is a built-in form of psychotherapy that encourages us, and sometimes forces us, to grow and develop as human beings. **A happy marriage is the basis for a strong society and the center of a strong, happy family.**

The first step in making a happy marriage is to grow up. Become an independent adult and learn to make yourself happy on your own. Learn how to be responsible and to relate effectively with others. Then find the right person to share your happiness with. If you're a mature, healthy and happy person you can trust your unconscious to help you select an appropriate mate. If you're not, then get that way before you think about planning a wedding. If need be, get into therapy. Don't marry because everybody else is doing it or because you're afraid to be alone, or because you need someone to take care of you.

Don't marry so someone can make you happy; that's your own job.

Once you do marry, work steadily and lovingly to accept your mate as is, to understand and appreciate how you are different, then to value and emulate those different ways of being and doing. Talk out your disagreements in a respectful, generous, and loving way. Be prepared to compromise. When you're wrong, admit it and apologize. Forgive your mate for not being perfect and extend that forgiveness to yourself. Don't dwell on the past. If you and your spouse can't work things out, get to a counselor, quickly. Make a true commitment to your spouse and your marriage– for life– and stick to it. And have some fun together.

A FINAL NOTE

The fact that you must *do* something to make yourself happy should not lead you to the mistaken belief that happiness should be the focus of your thoughts and actions. Happy people generally aren't thinking much about being happy. They're too focused on doing their jobs, playing their music, taking care of their kids or serving their God to dwell for long on the issue of happiness. If you asked them, "Are you happy?" they'd likely be a bit surprised. "I suppose I am," they might say; "I hadn't really thought much about it." Happiness is best approached indirectly. It is a byproduct of our thoughts and actions rather than a goal in itself. Find your life's passion and purpose and happiness will find you. So straighten out your thinking, reassess your priorities, and love your mate. Go make someone happy– **you.** In fact, make *two* someones happy by giving your spouse the gift of being married to a happy person, then working together to make both of you happy.

Appendix: The Rock and Roll Guide to a Happy Marriage:

As I'm talking with a patient, I often notice a tune playing in my head. If I pay attention to it, I usually find that there is something meaningful about the particular tune selected for me by my own unconscious mind. It's telling me something about the therapy. Most times it isn't especially earth-shattering, and often it's trivial or something I'm already aware of. But sometimes it tells me something I haven't yet consciously realized or confirms something I wasn't too sure of. Over the years I've come to value and trust these messages from my unconscious. I sometimes even share them with my patients, though I'm not much of a singer. My brother, also a therapist and more of a musician than I, does the same. Song has the power to convey messages in a particularly powerful way, perhaps because it so beautifully blends the verbal and nonverbal levels of communication. Its message tends to stick in your mind in a way words alone may not. So, in an effort to help you remember what we've learned about marriage– and just for the sheer fun of it– I present this rock-and-roll guide to a happy marriage. (Actually, some of the songs are more Pop than Rock, and some are Blues or Country, but let's not get too technical. I've listed the artist who sang them when I could remember who it was.)

"You can't always get what you want, but if you try, sometimes, you get what you need." (Mick Jagger and the Rolling Stones) No one person or one relationship can meet all your needs in life, and there is no perfect spouse. You won't always get your way in the marriage, and you will be called upon to compromise. But if you work at it, you can make yourself very happy with your spouse and get most of what you need.

"Time is bound to make us see just how good 'good enough' can be." (Bonnie Raitt) Over time you can discover that, while your mate isn't perfect, he or she is plenty good enough to be happy with.

"You can't have love, children, when you're keeping score." (Also Bonnie Raitt) Assessing the blame or nitpicking about who has made the biggest contribution to the marriage is destructive of the spirit of team play and cooperation essential to its survival. Both partners must be willing to sacrifice lovingly for the good of the family. Personally, I think this applies to money as well, and I advocate the one-pot approach to finances.

"Many a tear has to fall, but it's all in the game." (Tommy Edwards) If you get close to someone, you're bound to get hurt sooner or later. It's the price of admission to intimacy. **"Love hurts."** There are bound to be some tough times and some sadness in your marriage, even if it's a very good one. Honor your commitment and make it work in the long run.

"They say for every boy and girl there's just one love in this old world, and I know I've found mine." (Sonny James) This one is *not* true and must be remembered in the negative. There isn't just one perfect mate waiting out there for you, and there are many people you could make a happy marriage with, if you're willing to work at it. Selection of a good match is important, but work and commitment make love work in the long run. If you get it programmed correctly, your unconscious mind will help you select a good partner.

"Your mama ain't so bad, what happened to you?" (Carlos Santana) This is the flip side of **"I want a girl just like the girl who married dear old Dad."** Falling in love is a transference phenomenon in which you unconsciously relate to someone in the present by transferring feelings from the past, especially from your infantile relationship with your parents. This means you need to get yourself together, properly reprogram your unconscious, and use your head as well as your heart. **"You'd better shop around"** and not **"Get married in a fever."** (Johnny Cash)

"Wise men say only fools fall in love." (Elvis) This isn't true either, but it does make a point. Falling in love involves a lot of fantasy, and the wise person will think carefully before rushing into marriage. What do you really need from a marriage? What kind of person will make an appropriate spouse for you?

"I want a brave man; I want a cave man; Johnny show me that you care, really care for me." Some women mistake violence in men as strength, instead of recognizing it as a sign of weakness and insecurity. Some men think it is their job to control and dominate women, forcefully if necessary. Women need and respect a strong, confident man who can provide for and protect their families; they don't need an abusive tyrant.

"R-E-S-P-E-C-T, find out what it means to me." (Aretha Franklin) The key to effective communication in any relationship is respect. This is why you speak your mind assertively, not aggressively, avoid name-calling, and listen respectfully to your mate.

"Talk to me." (Sonny and the Sunliners) Good marriages thrive on good communication. Men, don't forget that conversation is a high-priority need for most women.

"Some people never say those words "I love you"; It's not their style to be so bold... but like a child they're longing to be told." (Paul Simon) Many people find it difficult to express love and affection, fearing to be rejected or embarrassed. But it is essential to marital harmony to be affectionate and express your love for each other. Take a chance and show some love. You might get some back in return.

"Maybelline, why can't you be true?" (Chuck Berry) Infidelity will wreck a marriage quicker than anything, including mothers-in-law, pets, even money. People have affairs for many reasons, but all of them are bad. If you're unhappy in your marriage, talk to your spouse about it, but don't confide in a girlfriend or boyfriend. **"Your cheating heart will tell on you."** (Hank Williams)

"To everything (turn, turn, turn,) there is a season." (The Byrds) Marriages go through predictable phases and stages of development. Don't panic when there's trouble, but work it through together. Marriages and families tend to break down at the transitions between these stages, if they don't negotiate them together, as a team.

"Oh, how happy you will be if you keep the Ten Commandments of Love." If you work on your marriage lovingly, maintain your commitment steadfastly, communicate respectfully, and sacrifice willingly, you will have a happy marriage and a happy life.

"I got nasty habits." (The Stones again.) Being happily married means learning to accept and value your spouse as is, taking the good with the bad, tolerating eccentricities or annoying habits. It also means **"You got to change your evil ways"** for the good of your marriage. (Santana)

"All I really need is good loving." (The Rascals) True, but not just in terms of sex. If you **"can't get no satisfaction"** (Stones) and can't **"feel like a natural woman"** (Aretha Franklin) you aren't likely to be very happy in your marriage. But married love isn't just sexual pleasure or emotion; it's also about behaving in a loving way and honoring your commitment.

ABOUT THE AUTHOR

Bob Wendorf, Psy.D. is a licensed Psychologist and Marriage and Family Therapist with over 25 years' experience. A graduate of Baylor University and the University of Illinois, he is now in private practice in Birmingham, Alabama. He is the author of several publications on family therapy and a frequent lecturer on the subject, as well as a guest on local television and radio programs.

Dr. Wendorf and his wife Margaret are the parents of two adolescent sons, Karl and Marc. When time allows, Dr. Wendorf makes himself happy as an avid Bonsai enthusiast and gardener.

Dr. Wendorf can be contacted by E-Mail at Psychsavvy@aol.com.